Connecting People with Jobs: Key Issues for Raising Labour Market Participation in Australia

This work is published under the responsibility of the Secretary-General of the OECD. The opinions expressed and arguments employed herein do not necessarily reflect the official views of OECD member countries.

This document and any map included herein are without prejudice to the status of or sovereignty over any territory, to the delimitation of international frontiers and boundaries and to the name of any territory, city or area.

Please cite this publication as:
OECD (2017), *Connecting People with Jobs: Key Issues for Raising Labour Market Participation in Australia*, OECD Publishing, Paris.
http://dx.doi.org/10.1787/9789264269637-en

ISBN 978-92-64-26962-0 (print)
ISBN 978-92-64-26963-7 (PDF)

The statistical data for Israel are supplied by and under the responsibility of the relevant Israeli authorities. The use of such data by the OECD is without prejudice to the status of the Golan Heights, East Jerusalem and Israeli settlements in the West Bank under the terms of international law.

Photo credits: Cover © Sergio77/Shutterstock.com

Corrigenda to OECD publications may be found on line at: *www.oecd.org/about/publishing/corrigenda.htm*.

Foreword

Giving people better opportunities to participate in the labour market improves well-being and strengthens economic growth. Better labour market and activation policies help countries to cope with rapid population ageing by mobilising potential labour resources more fully. Many OECD countries achieved record employment levels prior to the global financial crisis, but in all countries employment rates differ markedly across population groups. High unemployment and the weak labour market attachment of some groups in society reflect a range of barriers to working or moving up the jobs ladder. In many countries the crisis has accentuated long-standing structural problems that are causing these disadvantages. It is a major challenge for policy makers in the coming years to address these problems and make OECD labour markets and, thus, OECD economies more inclusive.

Therefore, the OECD Employment, Labour and Social Affairs Committee is carrying out a new set of reviews of labour market and activation policies to encourage greater labour market participation of all groups in society with a special focus on the most disadvantaged, who face the greatest barriers and disincentives to finding work. This includes a series of country studies, *Connecting People with Jobs*, which provides an assessment of how well activation policies help all groups to move into productive and rewarding jobs and, where appropriate, policy recommendations that could improve the situation.

This report on Australia is the third country study published in this series. It has a special focus on better mobilising Australia's labour resources through identifying Australia's unmet activation potential, highlighting that multiple barriers to employment might prevent certain population groups to participate more fully in the labour market. Good practice examples from other OECD countries provide insights on the type of policies and measures which could be developed for these population groups. The report was prepared by Kristine Langenbucher, Daniele Pacifico, Christopher Prinz (project leader) and Marieke Vandeweyer, economists in the Directorate of Employment, Labour and Social Affairs of the OECD. Statistical assistance was provided by Dana Blumin and editorial assistance by Gabriela Bejan. The report benefited greatly from discussions with other teams in the Directorate of Employment, Labour and Social Affairs that have worked on previous projects with Australia.

Table of contents

Figures

Tables

Acronyms and abbreviations

ABS	Australian Bureau of Statistics
ALMPs	Active Labour Market Programmes
CBA	Cost-Benefit Analysis
COAG	Council of Australian Governments
ECEC	Early Childhood Education and Care
ERA	Employment Retention and Advancement
ESAt	Employment Services Assessment
EU-SILC	European Union Statistics on Income and Living Conditions
FFWS	Fit for Work Service
GFC	Global Financial Crisis
HILDA	Household, Income and Labour Dynamics in Australia Survey
HMT	Her Majesty's Treasury
JSCI	Job Seeker Classification Instrument
LFS	Labour Force Survey
NEET	Not in Employment, Education or Training
PES	Public Employment Service
TIOW	Targeted Initiative for Older Workers (Canada)

Executive summary

Australia's economy and labour market has weathered the difficult economic circumstances of the past decade relatively well and employment rates of the population aged 15-64 years are now almost back at their 2008 peak of 73%. This is significantly higher a rate than the OECD average, though lower than in some of the vanguard countries. Importantly, Australia has quite high labour force participation and employment rates for some population groups, but not all. To increase overall participation and employment rates, it will be critical for Australia to better mobilise the unused labour resources of these groups. This is also critical in view of rapid population ageing in the coming decades.

This report draws on comprehensive policy analysis undertaken by the OECD in recent years in the context of a number of policy reviews including *Working Better with Age*; *Investing in Youth*; *Back to Work*; *Mental Health and Work*; *Sickness, Disability and Work*; *Closing the Gender Gap*; and the *Activation Policy* review. It uses this analysis to:

- Identify unmet labour resources in the Australian population;
- Summarise the challenges for Australia for particular underrepresented groups;
- Provide examples of good practice from other OECD countries which provide a yardstick or some ideas for further reform to inform the policy process in Australia.

Unmet labour resources in Australia are considerable and they are concentrated in a number of groups of the population: i) women with young children and in particular lone parents; ii) women more generally, especially older women; iii) people with a disability; iv) people with mental health conditions; v) disadvantaged youth; and vi) Indigenous Australians. Employment gaps are substantial in some cases. For women with a young child under age 5, for lone parents with a child under age 15 and for Indigenous Australians the employment gap is around 25 percentage points; for people with mental health conditions the gap is between 14 and 34 percentage points, depending on the severity of their mental illness; and for people with a disability the gap is close to 40 percentage points.

The underrepresentation of these groups has many roots, some of which are related to the abilities and preferences of the individual, a lack of labour demand, or structural factors in the policy setup and the way in which institutions function. Structural policy factors can be addressed most easily, and such change would have repercussions on other causes and parameters, thereby creating considerable room for an improvement in participation and employment rates.

Often multiple barriers to employment prevent certain population groups to participate more fully in the labour market. To substantiate this argument, this report applies a statistical segmentation method, which divides the target population into groups of individuals facing a similar combination of employment barriers, in order to quantify the different faces of joblessness and to identify the real barriers to employment. It focuses on employability barriers (lack of skills, limited work experience, care responsibilities and health problems), motivation barriers (potential to find a sufficiently-paid job and household income situation), and opportunity barriers (labour demand and labour market frictions). Some employability barriers are particularly frequent and affect between one-third and one-half of those currently outside the labour market or only marginally attached; these barriers include limited work experience, low skills and poor health. Many people face several barriers at the same time: roughly 20% face three employment barriers; about 50% face two such barriers; and another 20% just one. Only very few people with no or weak labour market attachment will not have any significant employment barriers.

Addressing multiple barriers requires a broad policy approach. Employment interventions alone will not be sufficient to bring underrepresented groups into the labour market. Many of them will need better integrated support that also addresses their health problems or their care responsibilities, and many will need support in several steps in order to develop their skills and work experience. This implies that activation policy will need to be broad and dig deep to bring more people into the labour market.

This situation is not unique to Australia. Most OECD countries face a similar situation but problems differ across them. No country has found a solution that can simply be copied, but much can be learned from policies and approaches of other countries. For example, paying more attention to care responsibilities as a major employment barrier is common in many countries whereas paying due attention to clients' health problems rarely is.

A non-exhaustive list of ideas, lessons and policy approaches from other countries that Australia could consider adopting includes:

- Early intervention and job-to-job transition support for displaced workers;
- Focus on sustainable outcomes in funding employment service providers;
- Mutual obligations for mature age jobseekers, in line with other age groups;
- Return-to-work support for workers at risk of long-term sickness absence;
- Improved sickness certificates through work-focussed certification guidelines;
- Strict work testing for lone parents coupled with provision of affordable childcare;
- Support for disadvantaged youth to complete education and transition to work;
- Mental health focus in workplace legislation and employment service provision;
- Closing the gender employment gap by facilitating a better work and life balance;
- Closing the employment gap between Indigenous and non-Indigenous Australians.

Australia is currently experimenting with applying a new priority investment approach to welfare in order to use public resources effectively and efficiently. There is a range of issues Australia needs to look into to get such an approach right. For example, broader costs and benefits beyond actuarial-financial considerations are important as is the focus on people currently not in the welfare system; these people may need help at some stage and if not helped at the right moment, they might be at high risk of needing greater and more costly interventions in the future. The analysis in this report suggests that any attempt to assure a wise use of scarce public resources needs to be broad enough to take account of the manifold employment barriers of those not or only weakly attached to the labour market. Any cost-benefit simulation used as a basis for employment and welfare spending decisions therefore must include areas such as health and childcare, to name just a few.

Chapter 1

The unmet activation potential of Australia's labour market

Australia's labour market has performed well over the past 15 years and its labour force participation rate continuously increased over this period and ranks well above the OECD average. While Australia was impacted less by the global financial crisis than most other OECD countries, the commodity price bust led to a deterioration of the labour market and it only started to recover as of 2015. Not all of Australia's states and territories and sub-regional levels have recovered to the same degree and retrenchments due to economic reason have again increased over the past years. Furthermore, the chapter identifies some unmet activation potential more generally in Australia's labour market. Mobilising this potential in the future will bring Australia's labour force participation closer to that seen in the OECD's vanguard countries. Areas of untapped potential are especially prime-age women, mature age workers, people with disabilities and mental health conditions, as well as Indigenous Australians.

The statistical data for Israel are supplied by and under the responsibility of the relevant Israeli authorities. The use of such data by the OECD is without prejudice to the status of the Golan Heights, East Jerusalem and Israeli settlements in the West Bank under the terms of international law.

Introduction

The Australian labour market has performed well over the past 15 years and the labour force participation and employment rates for the working-age population (15-64 years) are well above the OECD average. The Australian economy weathered the global financial crisis (GFC) better than most OECD countries. Nevertheless, key labour market indicators deteriorated and only since 2015, Australia's labour market has strengthened again with employment growth picking up and unemployment slowly falling. The recovery has, however, been uneven and employment still shows a downward trend and unemployment is still rising in a number of states and different regions within the states. Accordingly, retrenchments due to economic reasons remain high in some areas. More generally, there is still unmet potential in Australia to increase labour market participation to the levels seen in the OECD's vanguard countries in the medium to longer term. After a snapshot of the Australian labour market more generally, this chapter considers some important labour market groups, many of which are currently underrepresented in the labour market. Among them are prime-age women with children, people over age 55 – particularly women –, young people who are not in employment, education or training and not actively looking for work either, people with a disability, people with mental health conditions, and Indigenous Australians. While there is scope to increase labour market participation – i.e. the extensive margin –, there is also some leeway to increase labour market participation on the intensive margin through increasing the number of hours worked, as a high share of the workforce –especially prime-age women with children –, currently work part-time hours.

The Australian labour market context

The employment rate is recovering, but still lags behind its 2008 peak

The Australian labour market has performed well over the past 15 years compared with most other OECD countries. Since 2000, both the Australian labour force and total employment increased by 29%. Also the Australian labour force participation rate increased over these 15 years and at 77% in 2015 it ranks above the OECD average of 71%. This increase has been driven by more prime-age women (25-54 years) and older men and women (55-64 years) participating in the labour force. However, over the coming 40 years, labour force participation is expected to decline as a result of population ageing (Commonwealth of Australia, 2015). At the same time, the employment rate increased continuously, reaching 73% in 2008, 7 percentage points above the OECD average. Labour market conditions were generally improving throughout the OECD area during the pre-crisis period, but not as markedly as in Australia, which ranks high in an OECD-wide comparison of employment rates. The Australian economy was impacted by the GFC much less than most OECD countries. However, following the peak in the second quarter of 2008, the employment rate declined and, from 2011, was further hit by the commodity price bust. Since mid-2015 Australia's labour market has strengthened as employment growth has picked up again, with non-resource activity now driving employment growth (OECD, 2016a). In the third quarter of 2016, the employment rate for the population aged 15-64 years still lagged behind its peak in 2008 (Figure 1.1). As discussed further below, a number of vulnerable groups (i.e. disadvantaged youth, lone parents, people with a disability) have, however, not benefitted from these recent labour market improvements and there are also huge variations in regional labour market outcomes.

Figure 1.1. **Australia's employment rate ranks high in an OECD comparison, but still is not back at its 2008 peak level**

A. Employment rate for persons ages 15-64, 2008 and 2015

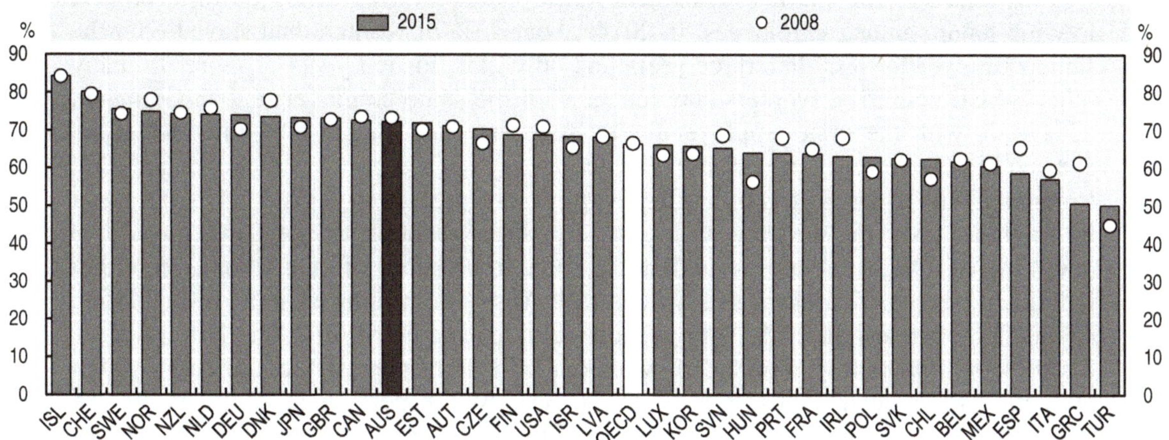

B. Employment rate for persons ages 15-64, selected OECD countries, Q1 2007 to Q3 2016

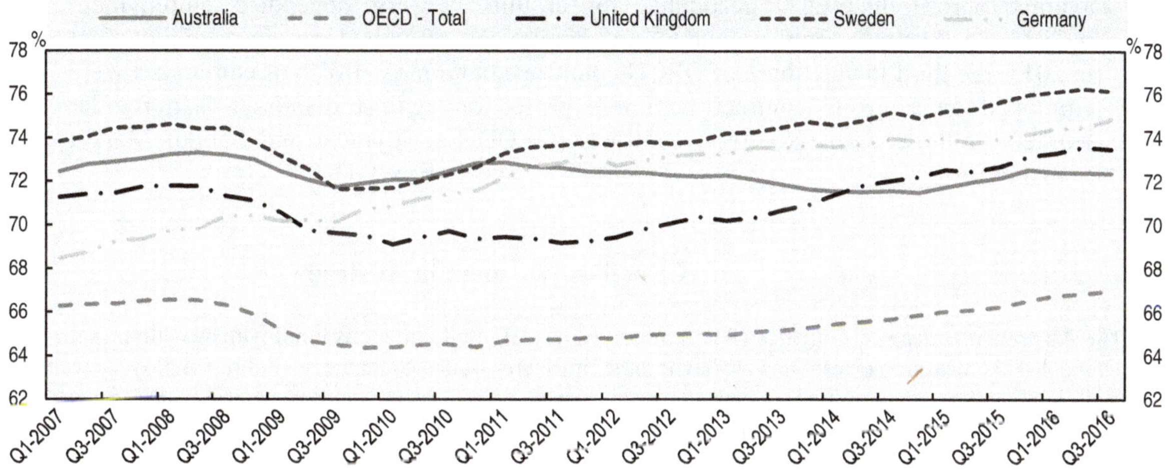

Source: *OECD Labour Force Statistics Database*, https://stats.oecd.org/Index.aspx?DataSetCode=LFS_SEXAGE_I_R (Panel A) and OECD Short-Term Labour Market Statistics, https://stats.oecd.org/Index.aspx?DataSetCode=STLABOUR (Panel B).

StatLink http://dx.doi.org/10.1787/888933447302

In Australia, high employment rates are associated with a high incidence of part-time employment, which was over 25% in 2015. Among OECD countries only the Netherlands and Switzerland have higher part-time shares. Part-time employment is not all voluntary: 23% of part-timers wished to work more hours in 2008, and this share increased to 29% by 2015. In 2015, involuntary part-time employment was 8.4% of the labour force, in comparison to an OECD average of 3.7% and this rate was only exceeded by crisis-hit Italy where the rate was 10.4%. Since 2002 involuntary part-time employment as share of the labour force has continuously exceeded the unemployment rate in Australia (*OECD Online Employment Database*, www.oecd.org/employment/database).

Australia has a flexible labour market, but almost a fifth of employees are employed on a casual basis

Australia's labour market is characterised by comparatively high job turnover and low job tenure among employees. In 2014, about 40% of workers had stayed with the same employer for less than three years and only 25% for ten years or more. In many other OECD countries, workers stay longer with the same employer; e.g. in Germany, 43% were with the same employer for at least ten years and in the United Kingdom 33% (*OECD Online Employment Database*, www.oecd.org/employment/database). Compared with other OECD countries, employment protection legislation is not strict in Australia. Over the past few years, largely since the onset of the GFC, more than one-third of OECD countries undertook some relaxation of regulations on either individual or collective dismissals. In contrast, Australia introduced some re-regulation of regular contracts in 2009 with the adoption of the Fair Work Act. Nevertheless, Australia still ranks low in an OECD-wide comparison of the strictness of employment protection for regular contracts (OECD, 2013a).[1] While permanent contracts are the prevalent form of dependent employment in OECD countries, the use of other types of contracts varies substantially across countries. Overall, fixed-term contracts are the prevalent forms of non-regular employment contracts in OECD countries and on average across the OECD accounted for around 11% of dependent employment in 2013. In Australia only around 6% of employees were in temporary employment in 2013, the third lowest share of OECD countries, but almost a fifth of employees were employed on a casual contract with less protection against dismissal than regular workers or those with fixed-term contracts (OECD Employment and Labour Market Statistics, http://dx.doi.org/10.1787/data-00297-en) (see Box 1.1).

Box 1.1. **Casual employment in Australia**

The Australian Bureau of Statistics (ABS) measures casual employment as employment without paid leave entitlements. This measure corresponds closely to other measures of casual status, including employees receiving a casual loading or self-identified casual status in survey data. Casual employees accounted for 19% of employees in November 2013, and made up a much larger share of employment in some industries, notably hospitality (65%), agriculture, forestry and fishing (47%), arts and recreation services (42%) and retail trade (40%). Around 55% of casual employees are women, and most casuals are employed in relatively low-skilled service occupations (ABS, 2013). Data from the Household, Income and Labour Dynamics in Australia (HILDA) survey, suggests that the proportion of employees being employed on a casual basis might be even higher: in 2014, 23% of employees claim to be casual workers.

Casual employees can be dismissed without notice or severance pay and generally have no legal right to regular or ongoing employment. They can also have their hours varied from week to week or day to day. In effect, casual employment is employment on an hourly or daily basis, although many casual employees work the same hours every week and may have long tenure in their jobs. Despite having no right to notice of termination, casual employees can make claims for unfair dismissal in the same way as regular workers. However, a period of service as a casual employee does not count towards the qualifying minimum employment period unless the casual worker was employed on a regular and systematic basis and had a reasonable expectation of continuing employment on that basis. In some industries, including construction, hospitality and some manufacturing sectors, employers must convert casual contracts to part-time or full-time contracts upon request if the employee has worked for a certain period of time and fulfilled criteria such as a minimum number of hours worked per week over the period of engagement. Typically, if a casual worker has been working regular hours for six or 12 months and requests to have their contract converted to a permanent full-time or part-time contract, employers cannot unreasonably refuse to do so.

Box 1.1. Casual employment in Australia *(cont.)*

Casual workers are typically not entitled to paid holiday or sick leave. However, they can access some forms of unpaid leave (e.g. up to two days per occasion to care for a sick family member or if a family member is gravely ill or dies). Casual employees who have worked at least 12 months for regular hours in the same job and who have a reasonable expectation of ongoing work can take up to 12 months of unpaid parental leave if they have or adopt a child.

In compensation for a lack of other entitlements, casual employees should receive a loading of around 25% on top of their hourly pay. In other regards, they should receive the same pay as other employees for doing the same work, including additional payments for working at non-standard times or on public holidays. In some industries, employers must pay casual employees for a minimum amount of work each time they are called in (e.g. three hours in the retail industry and two hours in the hospitality industry). Casual employees are also eligible to receive contributions to superannuation (Australia's private pension scheme) in the same way as other workers.

Source: ABS (2013), "Forms of employment, Australia", Australian Bureau of Statistics, Canberra, November, www.abs.gov.au/ausstats/abs@.nsf/mf/6359.0; and OECD (2014), "Non-regular employment, job security and the labour market divide", *OECD Employment Outlook 2014*, OECD Publishing, Paris, http://dx.doi.org/10.1787/empl_outlook-2014-7-en.

Albeit falling unemployment, the trend in rising long-term unemployed still has to be reversed

The post 2008 fall in employment rates in Australia is mirrored in an increase in unemployment since the onset of the GFC. While the unemployment rate declined in 2010 and early 2011, it increased thereafter again following the commodity price crisis, getting closer to the OECD average. The unemployment rate peaked in the first quarter of 2015, at 6.2%, and in the third quarter of 2016 it stood at 5.7% – still well above the trough of 4.1% in the first quarter of 2008 (Figure 1.2).

Figure 1.2. **Unemployment has started to fall in Australia, but is still above the 2008 trough**

Harmonised unemployment rate, percentage of total labour force (15 years and over), selected OECD countries, Q1 2007 to Q3 2016

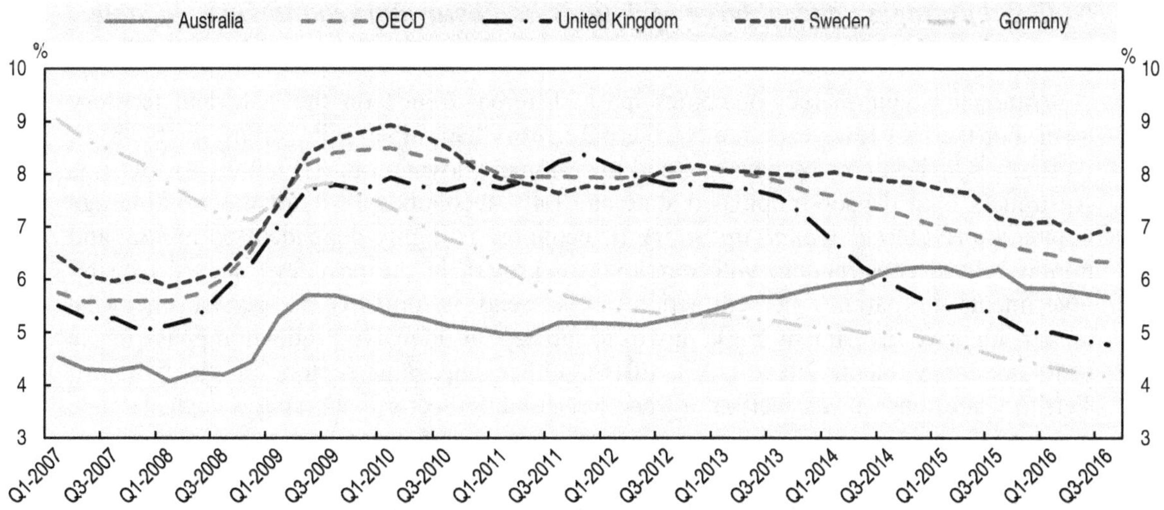

Source: OECD Short-Term Labour Market Statistics dataset, Harmonised Unemployment Rates http://stats.oecd.org//Index.aspx?QueryId=36324.

StatLink http://dx.doi.org/10.1787/888933447319

Following the increase in unemployment levels, the incidence of long-term unemployment (people unemployed for 12 months and more) also saw an increase in Australia from 2010 onwards. In 2015, almost a quarter of unemployed Australians have been unemployed for more than a year (Figure 1.3, Panel A). This is close to the high level 15 years ago, but still below the OECD average of around one-third. The risk of long-term unemployment is highest for mature age workers followed by prime-age workers: over a third of unemployed aged 50-64 years and around a quarter of those aged 30-49 years are long-term unemployed (Figure 1.3, Panel B).

Figure 1.3. **The trend of rising long-term unemployment has not yet been reversed in Australia**

People unemployed for more than one year as a share of all unemployed people: Australia and OECD, and Australia by age group, 2000-15

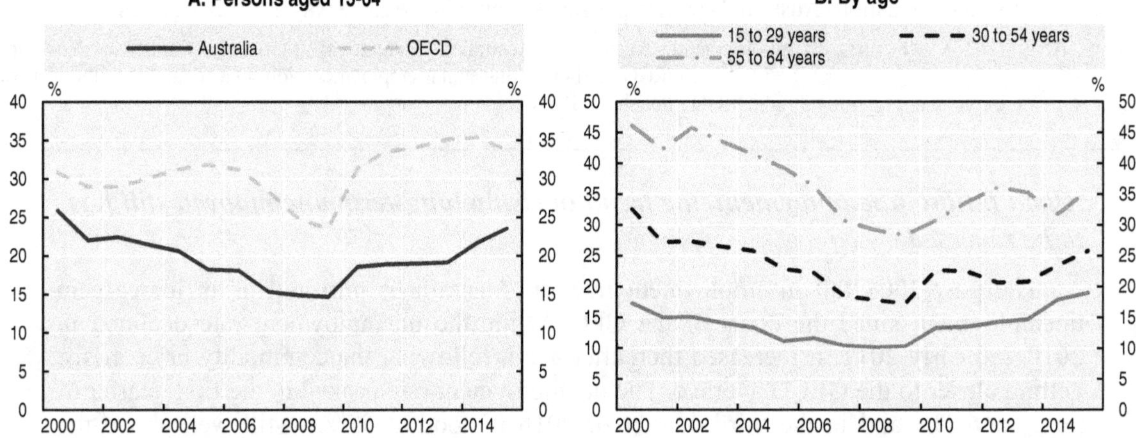

Note: OECD is a weighted average.

Source: *OECD Labour Force Statistics Database*, https://stats.oecd.org/Index.aspx?DataSetCode=DUR_I.

StatLink http://dx.doi.org/10.1787/888933447325

National averages conceal large variations in labour market outcomes on state and territory level

National labour market outcomes mask different trends on the state and territory level. For the past few years, the Northern Territory had, albeit with strong fluctuations, Australia's highest employment rate and lowest unemployment rate (Figure 1.4). But it is Australia's least densely populated state and only accounts for 1% of the working-age population (*OECD Regional Statistics*). Its economy is highly dependent on mining and mining-related construction, with employment growth in the past few years driven by investments in natural gas extraction. This trend is unlikely to persist once the labour-intensive investment phase moves to the capital-intensive production phase in the years to come (Kent, 2014; NAB, 2016). Other important sectors in the Northern Territory are tourism, as well as a very large public sector, including a high defence presence. Labour market outcomes, however, vary within the territory by location and different population groups. Unemployment is low in cities and towns like Darwin, Palmerston and Alice Springs, but high in remote areas like Barkly and the Central Desert (Department of Employment, 2016). As discussed in the last section of this chapter, labour market outcomes are also particularly poor for Indigenous Australians, who present nearly a quarter of the territory's population.

Figure 1.4. **Australia's labour market performance differs by state and territory**

Australian state and territory employment and unemployment rates, 2006-16

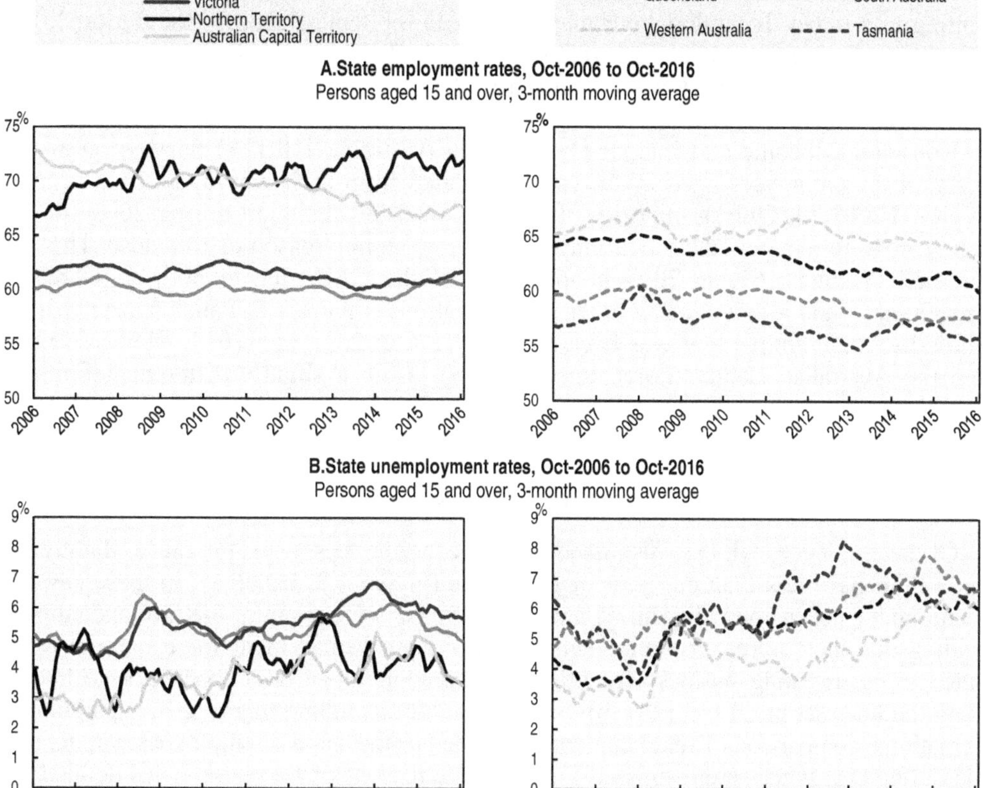

Source: Australian Bureau of Statistics, http://stat.data.abs.gov.au/.

StatLink http://dx.doi.org/10.1787/888933447330

A total of 57% of Australia's working-age population live in New South Wales and Victoria. The upward trend in the New South Wales labour market since 2015 has been relatively broad based, with unemployment rates in the rest of New South Wales largely closing the gap with the Greater Sydney area (Department of Employment, 2016). Employment growth over the past year was strongest in construction, professional services, and administrative and support services, while employment losses were largest in manufacturing, wholesale and retail trade (ABS, 2016). In Victoria employment growth by sector has been more evenly spread over past years, with the largest gains in health care and social assistance, professional services and wholesale trade, but larger losses in retail trade. The long-term downward trend in the manufacturing sector in Victoria halted somewhat, but is likely to pick-up again following the recent closure of the Ford Motor Company and General Motors Holden plants and the imminent closure of the Toyota Motor Corporation plants in 2017 (The Australian, 2016). The end of the mining boom is still taking its toll on Western Australia with employment rates declining and unemployment rates rising. A similar picture emerges for Queensland, even though unemployment fell in recent months. The decline in employment in South Australia has halted since early 2016 and unemployment rates fell. However, South Australia's unemployment rate still remains the highest in the nation. Tasmania has the lowest employment rate and its unemployment rate is close to that of South Australia (Figure 1.4).

Retrenchment rates are high in Australia, but most retrenched workers quickly find a new job

Labour turnover is relatively high in Australia compared with most OECD countries, pointing to a rather dynamic labour market. OECD job tenure data for the period 2011-12 indicate an average annual separation rate of 19.4%, against an OECD average of 16.6% (OECD, 2016b). However, only a minority of workers who separate from their jobs are retrenched by their employers for economic reason or for cause. Using data from the Household, Income and Labour Dynamics in Australia (HILDA) Survey, on average, 17.4% of the employees aged 20-64 years separated from their employers each year over the period 2002-14. Only a minority of workers who left their job during 2002-14, 3.8% each year, were retrenched by their employers for economic reason or for cause. This share increased to almost 6% in 2009 in the midst of the GFC, due to both an increase in retrenchments and a reduction in other job separations (Figure 1.5, Panel A). After having returned to 3.2% in 2011, it was back to nearly 5% in 2013 and 2014. More recent data from the Australian Labour Force Survey (LFS), using a slightly different definition of retrenchments, suggests a retrenchment rate of 5.3% in 2014-15 and 5.0% in 2015-16.[2] Consistent with the end of the mining boom mentioned above, retrenchment rates are above the national average in Western Australia and Queensland. Retrenchment rates are the lowest in the Australian Capital Territory and the Northern Territory (Figure 1.5, Panel B).

Of the employees who are dismissed due to economic reasons or for cause, slightly more than a third have less than one year of job tenure (Figure 1.5, Panel A). In these cases, job separation happened soon after hiring and may have been the result of the firm and employee deciding that they were not well-matched, rather than displacement for economic reasons related to deteriorating business conditions or the adopting of new production technology. Along the lines set in OECD (2013b), to avoid unduly including this type of separations, an international comparison of retrenchments is defined as the share of employees with tenure of at least one year who were dismissed for economic reasons or for cause. Thus defined, over the period 2002-14, 2.4% of Australian employees with tenure of at least one year were displaced each year on average, with a minimum of 1.7% in 2008 and a maximum of 3.6% in 2009. The impact of the GFC was important, but did not last long, as the displacement rate was back to 2.2% in 2011. In 2013 and 2014, however, the displacement rate increased strongly again, to 3.1%. Compared with other OECD countries where displacement is defined and measured in the same way, i.e. self-defined based on household panel data, displacement rates are relatively high in Australia (Figure 1.5, Panel C).

In Australia, a large share of displaced workers rapidly finds another job following displacement: over the period 2002-14 on average almost 70% of retrenched workers are re-employed within one year, and almost 80% within two years (Figure 1.5, Panel D). The OECD Back-to-Work project has assembled re-employment rates for displaced workers for a number of OECD countries using comparable time periods, samples of workers and definitions of displacement. By comparison with other OECD countries for which data are available, re-employment rates are relatively high in Australia, both in the first and the second year after displacement (OECD, 2016b). This reflects the relatively good labour market situation described above and probably also the relatively flexible nature of the Australian labour market. As in other countries hit by the GFC, re-employment rates in Australia fell during the GFC. The share of displaced workers re-employed within one year declined from 74% in 2008 to 58% in 2010. With the rapid rebound in labour market conditions, first-year re-employment rates were already back to 62% in 2011, increasing to 69% in 2013. First-year re-employment rates, however, significantly declined in 2014 to 53%, the lowest level for the period 2002-14 (Figure 1.5, Panel D).

Figure 1.5. **The incidence of retrenchments in Australia and outcomes following retrenchment**

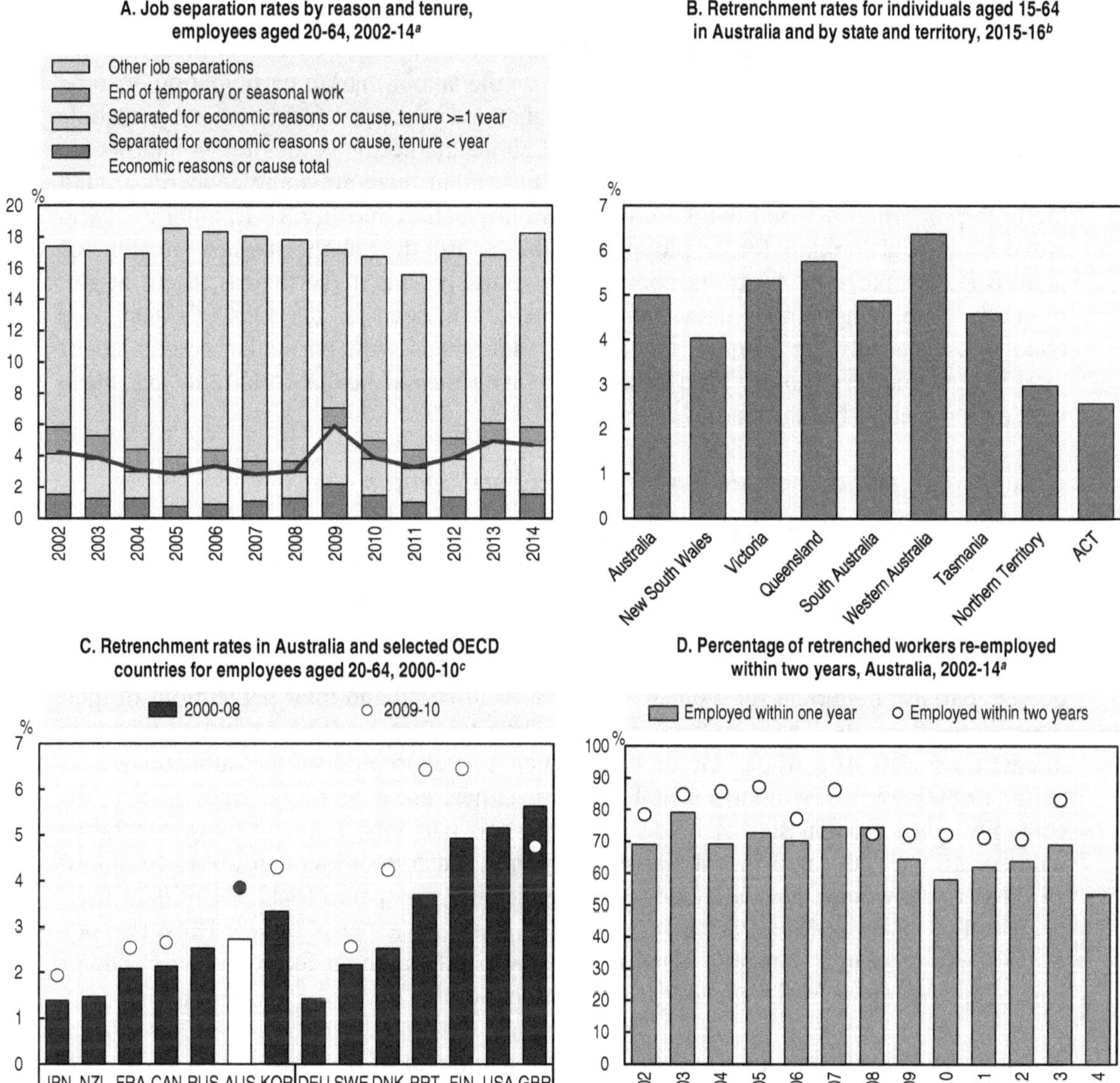

ACT: Australian Capital Territory.

a) Employees who were retrenched for economic reasons or for cause from their last job. 2002 to 2014 refer to the Australian financial years (which run from 1 July to 30 June) 2001/02 to 2013/14.

b) The figures include employees who were retrenched in any job held in the three months prior to the survey reference week, as well as self-employed persons whose business closed down for economic reasons. Data cover the period June 2015 to May 2016.

c) Employees with at least one year of tenure who are displaced from one year to the next. Data refer to 2002-13 for Australia. Unlike for the other countries, multiple job holders are included for Australia; it does not significantly affect the results as it consistently reduces retrenchment rates by 0.1 percentage point.

Source: Panels A and D: OECD estimates based on data from the Household, Income and Labour Dynamics in Australia (HILDA); Panel B: Australian Bureau of Statistics (2016), Labour Force, Australia, Detailed, Quarterly, August, Table 29a and Panel C: HILDA for Australia and for all other countries OECD (2013), "Back to work: Re-employment, earnings and skill use after job displacement", Final Report, Directorate for Employment Labour and Social Affairs, OECD Publishing, Paris, October, www.oecd.org/els/emp/Backtowork-report.pdf.

StatLink http://dx.doi.org/10.1787/888933447341

How does the labour market situation of specific groups in Australia compare internationally?

While Australia generally compares favourably in a cross-OECD comparison for labour market participation, there is scope to raise the labour market participation of some groups in the labour market. This section finds that one of the greatest untapped potentials is inactive and/or part-time working women. Labour market outcomes for young people in Australia are better than in most OECD countries, but there are some concerns around the high proportion of youth who are not in employment, education or training and who are not actively looking for employment either. Also the labour market situation of mature age workers in Australia compares favourably, but, nevertheless, there is still room for improving employment rates to the levels seen in the OECD's vanguard countries, especially for women. In contrast, individuals with particularly poor labour market outcomes are those with a disability or with mental health conditions and those with an Indigenous background.

Untapped potential: Female labour market participation

Realising women's professional potential in the labour market benefits the Australian economy. OECD projections suggest that GDP would increase by 12% over the next 20 years if labour force participation rates among women in OECD countries reached male levels (OECD, 2012). Taking the perspective of women and their families, work is not only the main source of income and, hence, economic security for most people, but also important for women's personal well-being and their perceptions of their overall quality of life. These, in turn, influence their families' well-being and also have an impact on society as a whole. Given that women's levels of educational attainment now match or outpace men's in most OECD countries, there are potentially large losses to the economy when women stay at home or work short part-time hours. Young Australian women are well-educated in comparison to young Australian men: in 2014, 53.7% of 25-34 year-old women have attained tertiary education, compared to 42.5% of their male peers (OECD Gender Data Portal, www.oecd.org/gender/data/education/). However, one of the areas of greatest untapped potential in the Australian labour force is inactive and/or part-time working women, especially those with children.

More prime-age women could enter the labour market in Australia

The employment rate of prime-age women (aged 25-54 years) grew by 5.5 percentage points over last 15 years and now stands at 72.5%. Nevertheless, female employment in Australia still ranks in the lower third of OECD countries as Figure 1.6 shows (Panel A). While for men full-time work still is the norm across the OECD, the proportion of women working full-time varies considerably across OECD countries. In Hungary, 94% of prime-age women work full-time, whereas only 40% of prime-age women in the Netherlands do so. Also in Australia a high proportion of prime-age women work part-time (less than 30-usual weekly hours of work in the main job); only Switzerland, Netherlands, Austria and Germany have higher shares of women working part-time (Figure 1.6, Panel B).

Figure 1.6. **Female employment increased over the past 15 years, but more than a quarter of women work part-time in Australia**

A. Employment rate for prime-age women, (25-54), 2000 and 2015

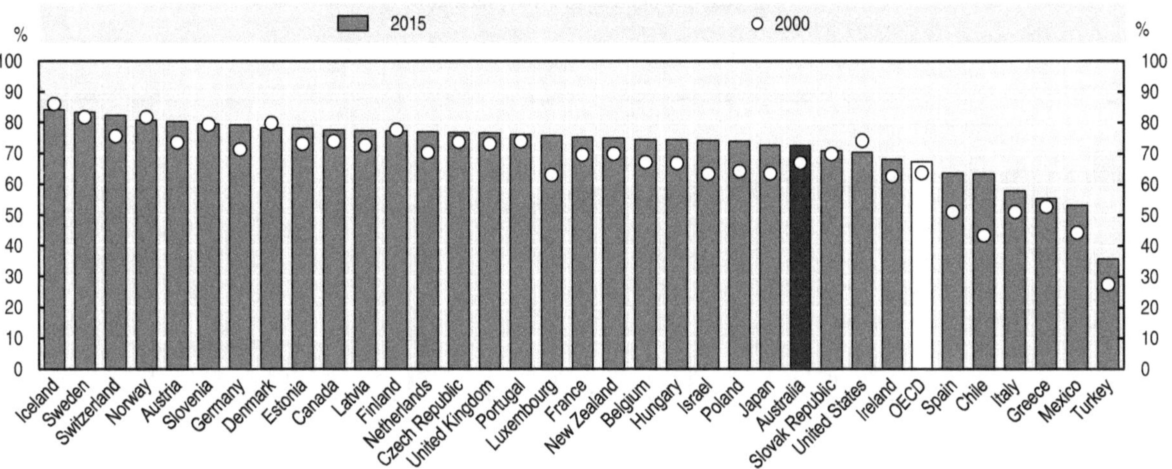

B. Share of full-time and part-time employment for prime-age women, (25-54), 2015

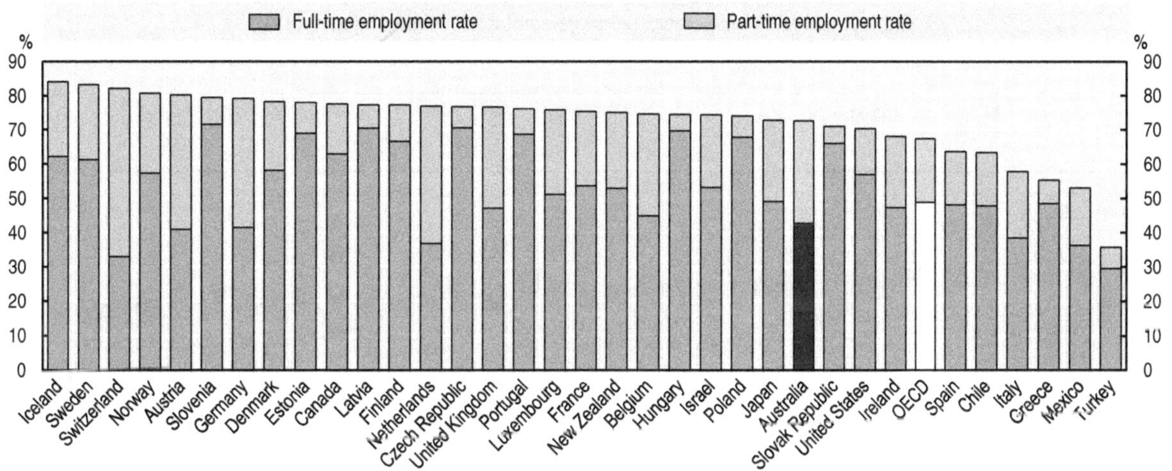

Source: *OECD Labour Force Statistics Database*, https://stats.oecd.org/Index.aspx?DataSetCode=LFS_SEXAGE_I_R (Panel A) and Incidence of FTPT employment - national definitions, https://stats.oecd.org/Index.aspx?DataSetCode=FTPTN_I (Panel B).

StatLink http://dx.doi.org/10.1787/888933447359

In Australia, motherhood has a strong impact on labour market participation

Having children has an impact on parental labour market participation. The impact on women is usually much stronger than that on men, especially when children are young. Often traditional gender roles and patterns prevail, but maternity leave and parental and home care leave entitlements also play a role. Hence, on average in the OECD, employment rates of women with children are lower than those of all prime-aged women (i.e. those aged 25-54 years) without a child. While in many countries the difference is rather small, in Australia, the gap is almost 9 percentage points (Figure 1.7, Panel A).

Figure 1.7. **Australian women with dependent children, especially very young ones, have particularly low employment rates**

A. Employment rates for women (25-54 years old) with *no children* and *at least one child* aged 0-14[a] years, 2014[b]

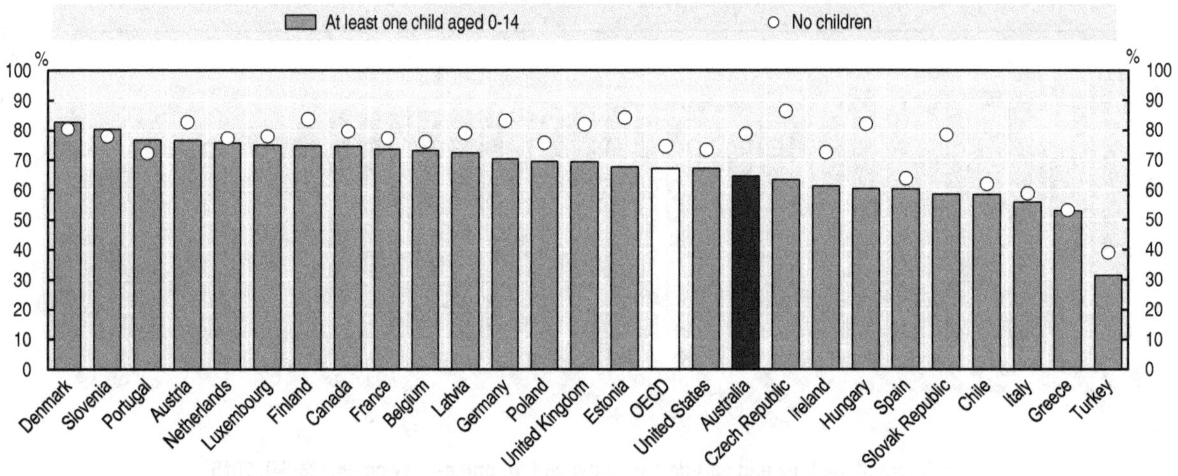

B. Employment rates for women[c] (25-54 years old) with children (aged 0-14[a]) by age of youngest child[d], 2014[b]

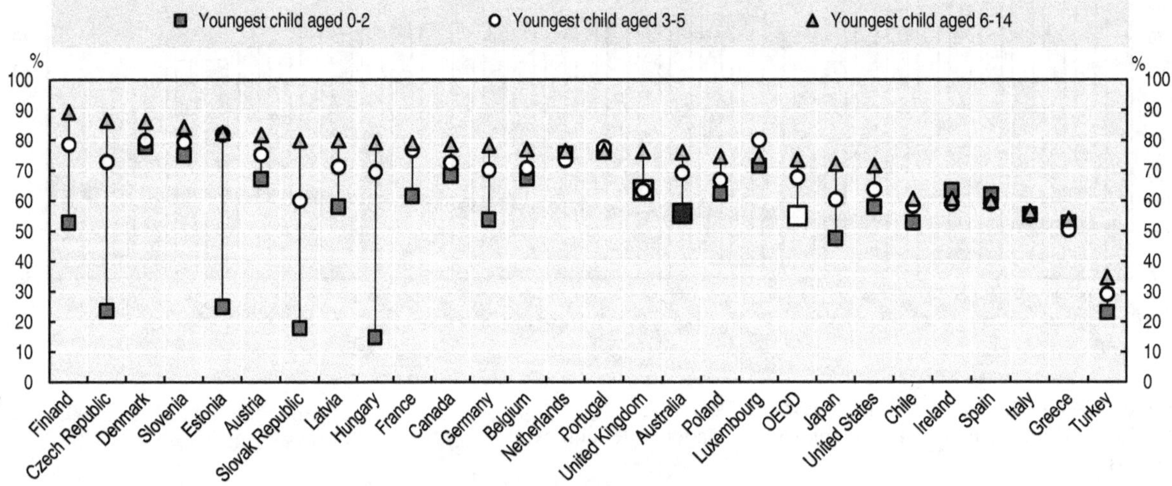

Note: OECD is an unweighted average across the OECD countries in each panel.

a) For Canada, children aged between 0-15 and 0-17 for the United States.

b) Data for Denmark and Finland refer to 2012, and to 2013 for Chile, Germany and Turkey.

c) For Australia, data refer to "Wives/Partners" and not mothers.

d) For Australia, children aged between 0-4, 5-9 and 10-14. For Canada the age group 6-14 refers to 6-15 and to 6-17 for the United States.

Source: *OECD Family Database*, www.oecd.org/els/family/database.htm; and ABS, Labour Force, Australia: Labour Force Status and Other Characteristics of Families, June 2015 for Australia (Panel B).

StatLink http://dx.doi.org/10.1787/888933447363

In most OECD countries employment rates increase with the age of the youngest child. While Australia's employment rate for mothers with very young children ranks towards the lower end, the situation seems to improve for women with older children (Figure 1.7, Panel B). However, it should be noted that employment rates reported for Australia are likely to be biased upwards, as all three categories include older children than for most other countries shown (see Notes of Figure 1.7).

While mothers not in the labour force are an untapped potential in the Australian labour force, there is also a great untapped potential among mothers working part-time only. Recent analysis by the OECD shows that among partnered working mothers (aged 25-45 years) in Australia 45% work part-time, four-fifth of them cite family reasons as the main reasons for doing so, and they work very short hours on average (OECD, 2016c). Average usual weekly hours of partnered mothers working part-time in Australia are less than 20 hours, the second lowest number in the OECD. Only in Belgium, Iceland, France, Sweden and Denmark, part-time working mothers work 25 or more hours per week (Figure 1.8). In these countries, longer working hours of mothers are supported through comprehensive formal childcare and pre-school services for under-school age children as well as out-of-school-hours care services for children of primary school age (*OECD Family Database*, www.oecd.org/social/family/database.htm).

Figure 1.8. **Partnered mothers in Australia work very short part-time hours**

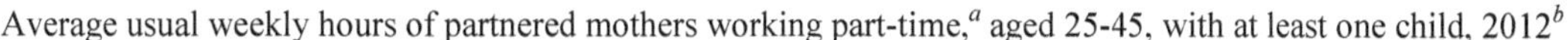

Average usual weekly hours of partnered mothers working part-time,[a] aged 25-45, with at least one child, 2012[b]

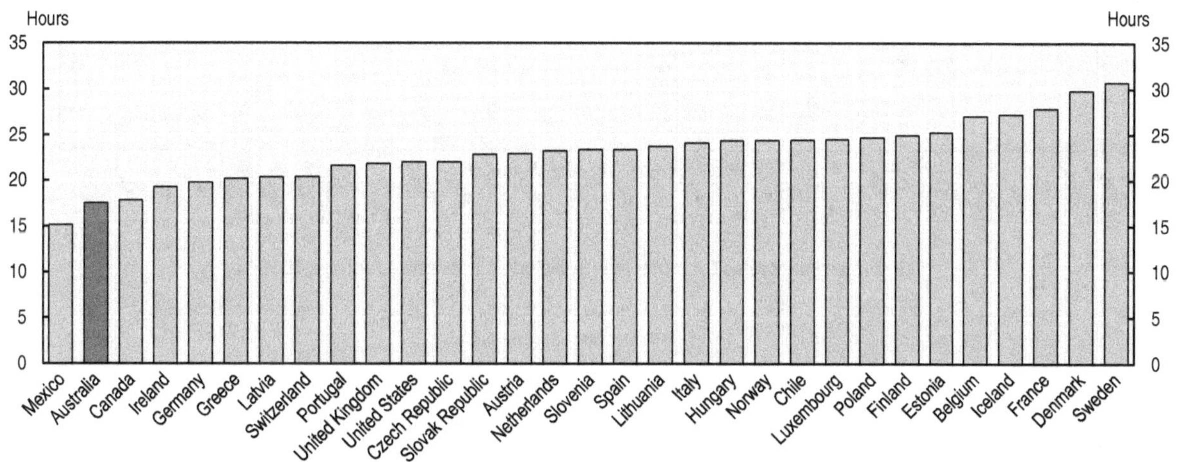

Note: Usual working hours of the (self-)employed for European countries, actual hours worked for Chile and Mexico. Data refer to total hours worked in al jobs except for Chile where only hours worked in the main job are considered.

a) The distinction between part-time and full-time is self-defined, i.e., based on respondents' own perceptions of whether they are in part-time or full-time employment. Part-time status based on weekly working hours below 30 hours for Australia, Canada and Mexico.

b) Data refer to 2011 for Canada, to 2013 for Chile and to 2014 for Australia, Mexico and the United States.

Source: OECD (2017), *Dare to Share: Germany's Experience Promoting Equal Partnership in Families*, OECD Publishing, Paris, http://dx.doi.org/10.1787/9789264259157-en.

StatLink http://dx.doi.org/10.1787/888933447372

The labour market participation of lone mothers is particularly low

Lone parents head over a tenth of Australian households but they have very low labour market participation (*OECD Family Database*, www.oecd.org/social/family/database.htm). Australia, along with a number of other OECD countries with low lone parent employment rates – New Zealand and the United Kingdom – has reformed its welfare system to encourage more lone parents to take up work. The 2006 Welfare to Work reform introduced participation requirements for principle carer parents when the child turns six or seven. Consequently, the employment rate of sole mothers increased from 46.1% in 2004 to 57.2% in 2008, but it fell back to 50.8% in 2014. Australia's lone mother employment rate in 2014 is still the third-lowest in the OECD, after Ireland and Turkey (Figure 1.9, Panel A). Further welfare reforms for lone parents were introduced in 2013 and may impact on lone parent employment rates in the years to come (see Chapter 3), but they are unlikely to bring Australia close to the OECD average.

Figure 1.9. **Labour market outcomes of lone parents are especially low in Australia**

A. Employment rates for mothers (15-64 year olds[a]) with at least one dependent child aged 0-14[b], by partnership status, 2014[c]

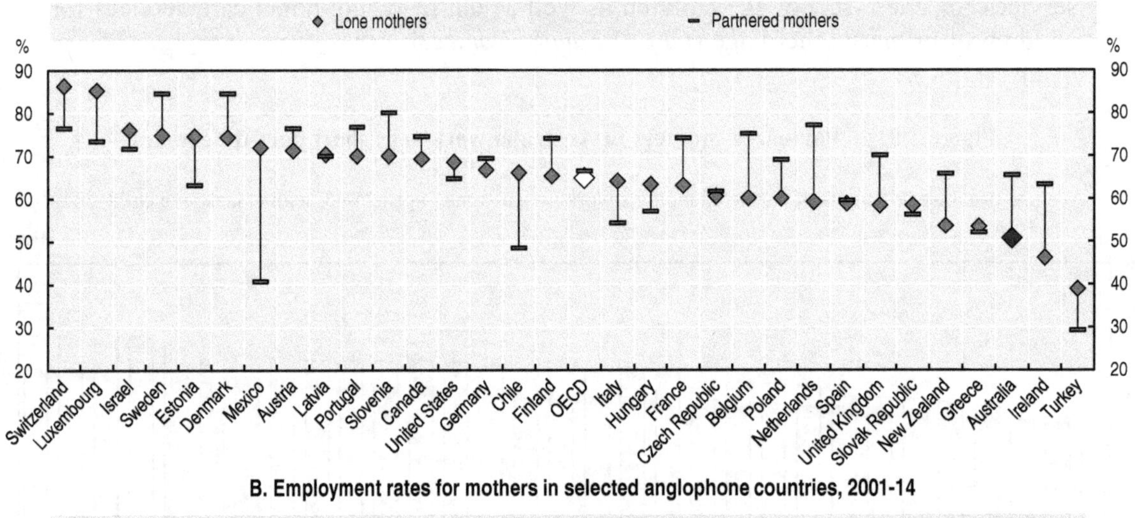

B. Employment rates for mothers in selected anglophone countries, 2001-14

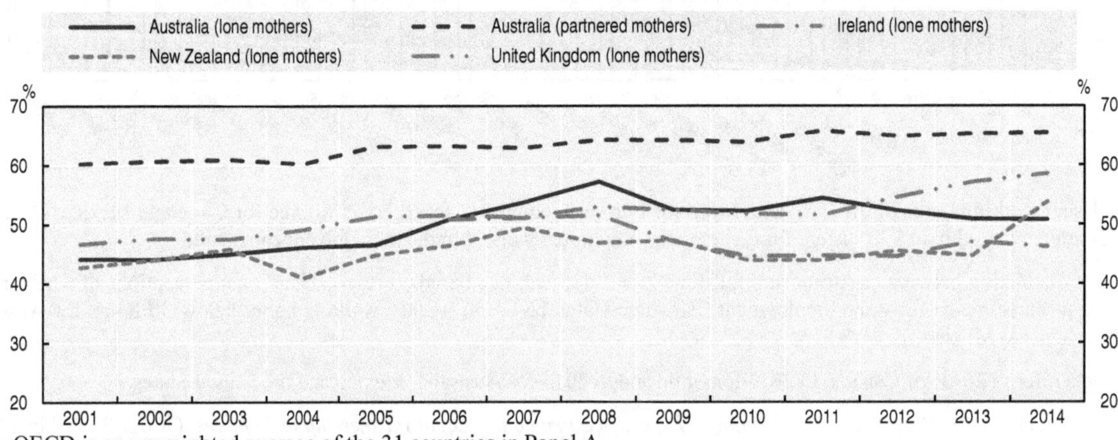

Note: OECD is an unweighted average of the 31 countries in Panel A.

a) For Sweden, women aged 15-74.

b) For Canada, children aged between 0-15 and 0-17 for the United States.

c) Data for Denmark and Finland refer to 2012, and to 2013 for Chile, Germany and Turkey.

Source: *OECD Family Database*, www.oecd.org/els/family/database.htm.

StatLink http://dx.doi.org/10.1787/888933447385

Comparing the employment rate of lone mothers with that of partnered mothers in Australia suggests the labour market slack over recent years impacted lone mothers most (Figure 1.9, Panel B), possibly because of the type of jobs they hold. Lone mothers are more often employed in low and middle skilled occupations, which have experienced weaker employment growth over recent years. Employed lone mothers are also more concentrated in declining and low-growth sectors (e.g. manufacturing, retail trade). Furthermore, the proportion of lone mothers employed on a casual basis (41%), where they enjoy little employment protection (see Box 1.1), is more than double the rate for partnered mothers (19%) in 2014.[3]

Labour market and education outcomes for Australian youth are better than in most OECD countries

The youth employment rate in Australia has consistently been above the OECD average over the last 30 years and increasingly so since the mid-1990s (OECD, 2016b). The high youth employment rate is driven by the fact that Australia has one of the highest proportions of students combining work and study: over 60% of students worked in 2012 (OECD, 2015a). However, in Australia, as for youth across the OECD, employment rates declined with the onset of the GFC and, at 65.5% in 2015, the employment rate of the 15-29 year-olds was still 4.3 percentage points below its peak in 2008 (Figure 1.10).

Figure 1.10. **Australian youth have relatively high employment rates compared internationally**

Youth (ages 15-29) employment rates, 2008 and 2015

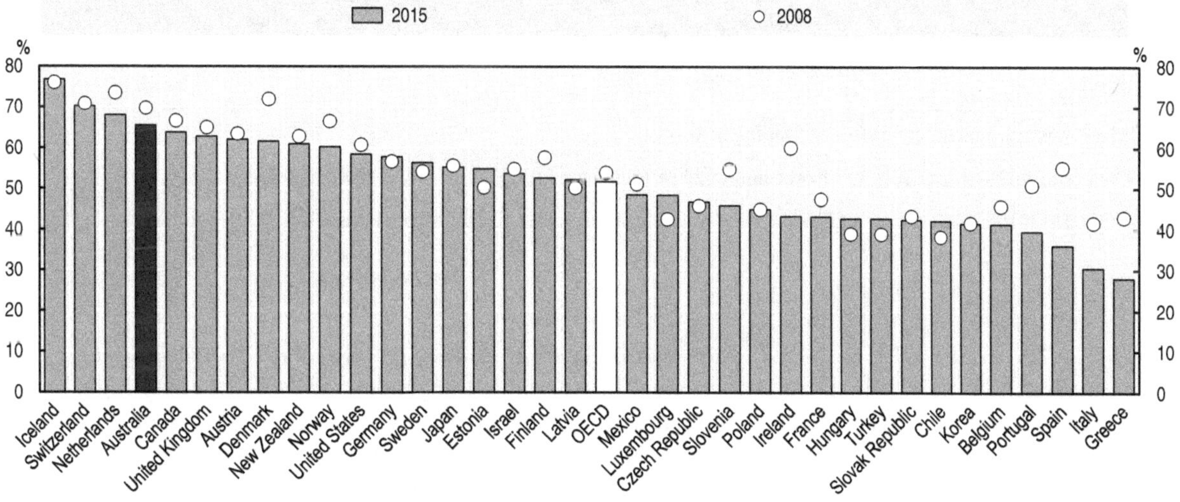

Source: *OECD Labour Force Statistics Database*, LFS by sex and age - indicators, http://stats.oecd.org//Index.aspx?QueryId=54218.

StatLink http://dx.doi.org/10.1787/888933447394

The number of Australian youth not in employment, education or training (NEET) reached about 580 000 individuals in 2015. The Australian NEET rate stood at 11.8% compared to 14.5% across the OECD (Figure 1.11). With a large fraction of NEETs being 'inactive' (i.e. not actively looking for work and not in the labour force) across the OECD, it is important to look beyond unemployment rates to assess the labour market situation of young people. This is important in countries like Australia, where NEET rates are relatively low but the share of inactive young people amongst NEETs is relatively high. In Australia, more than two-thirds of NEETs are out of education or work and not actively looking for employment (Figure 1.11) because of barriers to education and employment which many of these young people face. Low educational attainment is an important driver of NEET status, in Australia as in other OECD countries, often related to barriers such as health problems or care responsibilities. Youth with at-most lower secondary education (Year-10 Certificate or equivalent) account for more than one out of three NEETs, and their risk of being NEET is three times as high as for those with tertiary education (OECD, 2016b).

Figure 1.11. **Australia's NEET rate is lower than the OECD average**

NEET rates, age 15-29, 2015

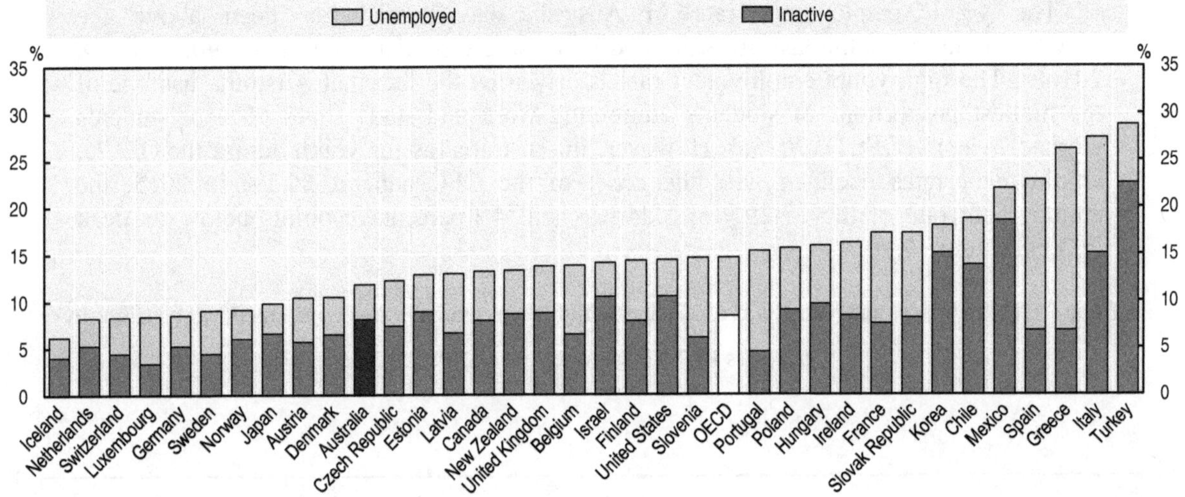

NEET: Not in employment, education or training.

Note: Data refer to 2013 for Chile and Korea and to 2014 for Japan. OECD is an unweighted average.

Source: OECD (2016), *Education at a Glance 2016, OECD Indicators*, OECD Publishing, Paris http://dx.doi.org/10.1787/eag-2016-en.

StatLink http://dx.doi.org/10.1787/888933447402

Across the OECD, NEET rates exhibit a clear gender pattern, with women having persistently higher NEET rates than men. In Australia, the gender gap is particularly high: NEET rates are 36% higher for women than men across the OECD – in Australia, the gap in NEET rates is 51%. In Australia having a young child is the main driver of gender differences in NEET rates. Overall, just 15% of female youth have a child under age 5 but this group accounts for just under half of female NEETs. Australia's relatively high childcare costs are one important factor contributing to the high NEET rates among young mothers with young children. Within Australia, NEET rates vary strongly by state and territory. NEET rates are close to half the countrywide average in the Australian Capital Territory, while they are twice as high as the average in the Northern Territory. NEET rates also differ by the remoteness of the location, driven entirely by higher NEET rates for Indigenous youth in remote areas. Overall, NEET rates are more than three times higher for the Indigenous population compared to the non-Indigenous population (OECD, 2016b).

The Australian education system performs well overall: education completion rates are high and the share of young adults with below upper-secondary education has fallen substantially in recent years so that it is now below the OECD average: in 2014, 13% of Australian 25-34 year-olds had not completed upper-secondary education compared to an OECD average of 17%. This figure has strongly declined from a level of 32% back in 2000. But disadvantaged students do not do as well: youth from low socio-economic background, those living in remote areas and Indigenous youth are less likely to complete Year 12 and also perform substantially worse in literacy and numeracy tests (OECD, 2016b).

Room for improvement: Labour market participation of mature age workers

In most OECD countries, employment rates for mature age workers have been growing over the past 15 years. In Australia, the employment rate for those aged 55-64 years grew from 46.1% in 2000 to 62.1% in 2015, outpacing the growth of the OECD on average, where employment rates for the same age group grew from 47.5% to 58.1%. With a few exceptions, employment rates for mature age workers across the OECD also continued to increase during the recent downturn, in contrast to the rates of young and prime-age workers in many OECD countries. In Australia, employment rates for mature age workers increased by 4.8 percentage points since the beginning of the GFC (Figure 1.12, Panel A).

The employment rate for those aged 55-59 years in Australia is around the OECD average. More Australians, however, continue working past 59 years than for example older people in Denmark, Finland, the United Kingdom, and Netherlands, which have higher employment rates for the age-group 55-59 years than Australia. Accordingly, Australia has a higher employment rate for persons aged 60-64 years than those countries. However, there is still room to increase employment rates to the levels seen in vanguard countries like Iceland, Japan, Norway and New Zealand (Figure 1.12, Panel B). Owing to the lower labour market participation of women in comparison to many other OECD countries, Australia also has a relatively large gender gap in employment for those aged 55-64 years.

The unemployment rate is structurally lower for persons aged 55 years and over than for younger persons (Figure 1.13, Panel A and also Figure 1.2). By contrast, the steadily growing share of mature age workers in the working-age population since 2000 and their increased presence on the labour market have translated into an increase in the proportion of older persons among the unemployed: at the end of 2015, 10.8% of the unemployed were aged 55 years and over in Australia, compared to 6.7% in 2000. Similar developments are seen across the OECD, where on average the share of older persons among the unemployed increased from 9.7% in 2000 to 13.2% in 2015.

While the mature age worker unemployment rate is lower than the unemployment rate for prime-age workers across the vast majority of OECD countries, mature age workers have greater difficulty in escaping unemployment and Australia is no exception. In Australia in 2015, 35.7% of unemployed persons 55-64 were long-term unemployed (i.e. unemployed for more than a year), compared to 46.8% in the OECD on average (Figure 1.13, Panel B). The rate of long-term unemployment among older unemployed is about 10 percentage points higher than that of the prime-age unemployed (compare Figure 1.3).

Figure 1.12. **Employment rates for mature age workers in Australia are above the OECD average, but there is further room for improvement**

A. Employment rates for persons aged 55-64 years, OECD countries, 2000, 2008 and 2015

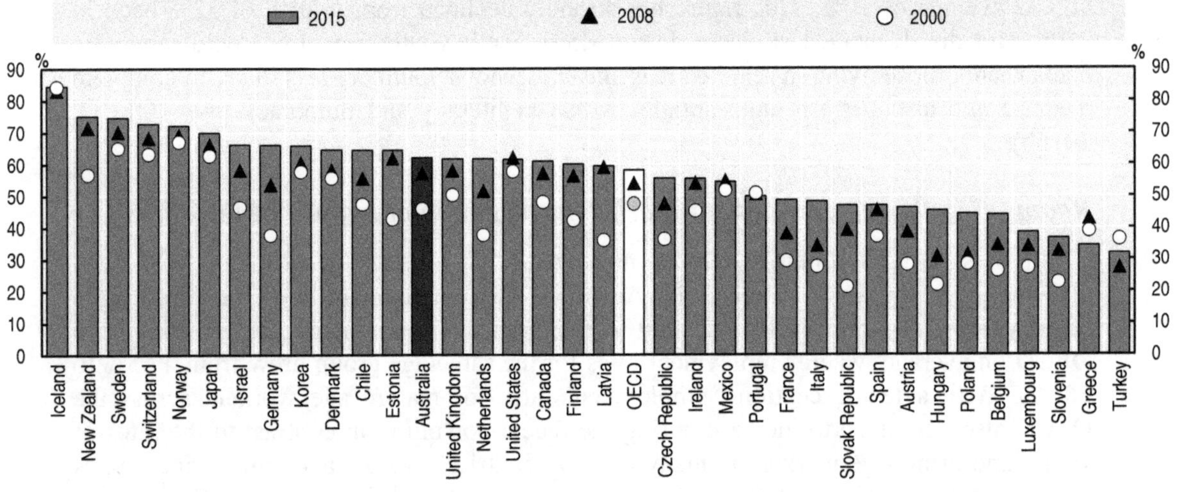

B. Employment rates for elderly persons (55-69) as a percentage of the age group, OECD countries, 2015

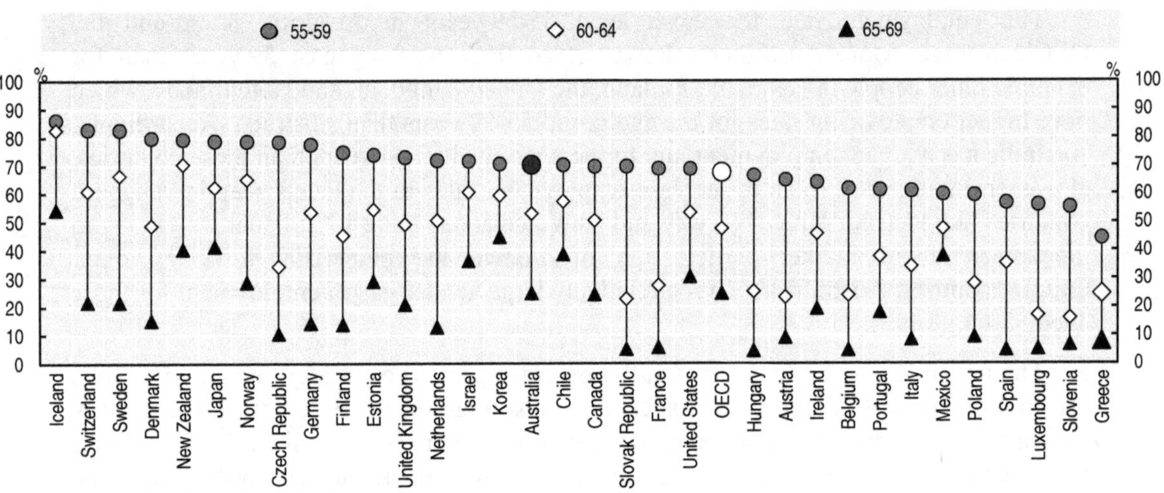

Source: *OECD Labour Force Statistics Database*, LFS by sex and age - indicators, http://stats.oecd.org//Index.aspx?QueryId=54218.

StatLink http://dx.doi.org/10.1787/888933447418

Figure 1.13. **The older unemployed in Australia fare better than the OECD average**

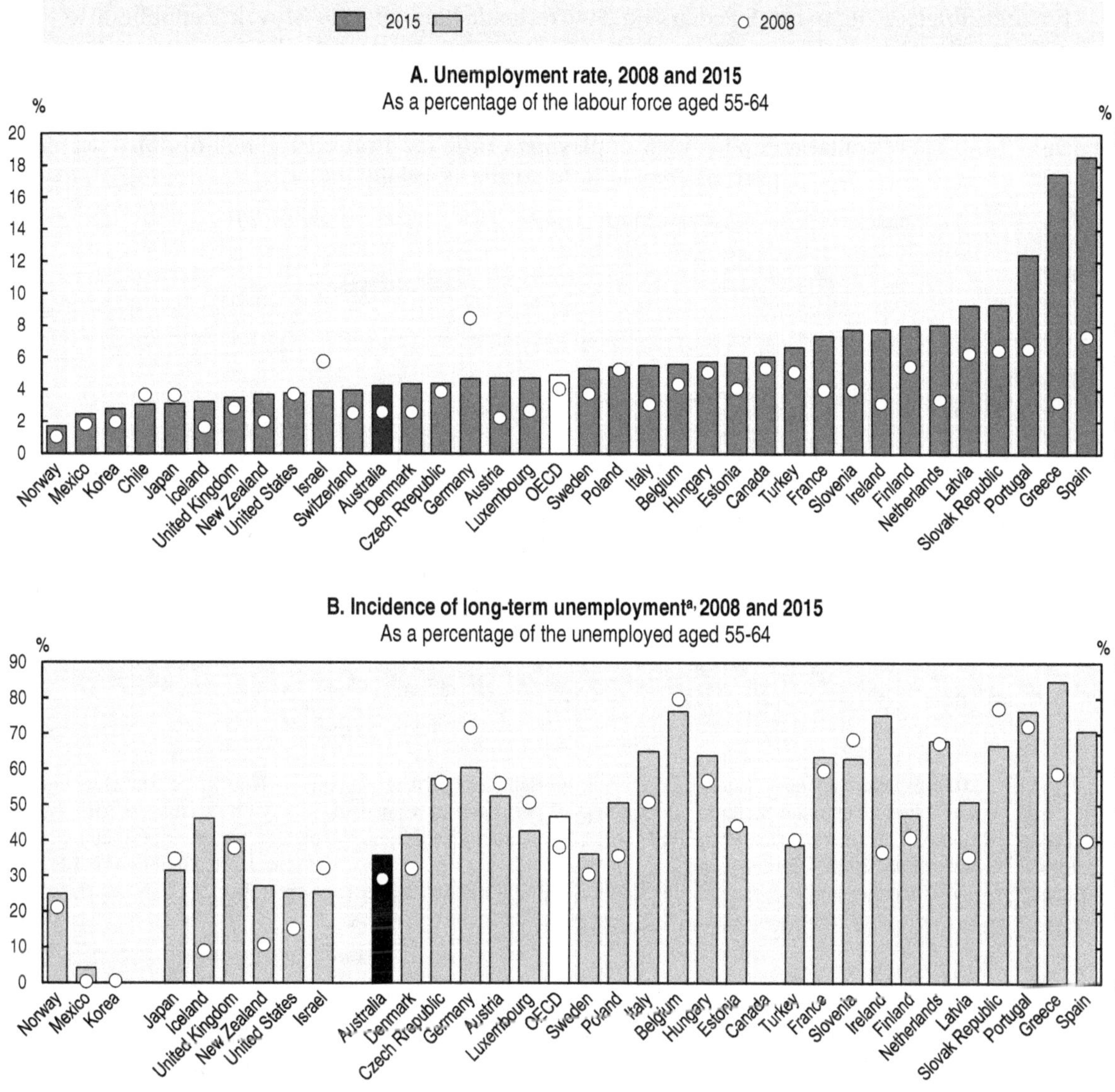

A. Unemployment rate, 2008 and 2015

As a percentage of the labour force aged 55-64

B. Incidence of long-term unemployment[a], 2008 and 2015

As a percentage of the unemployed aged 55-64

a) Unemployed for more than one year.

Source: *OECD Labour Force Statistics Database*, LFS by sex and age – indicators, http://stats.oecd.org//Index.aspx?QueryId=54218 (Panel A); Incidence of unemployment by duration http://stats.oecd.org//Index.aspx?QueryId=9593 (Panel B).

StatLink http://dx.doi.org/10.1787/888933447427

People with a disability have not profited from the positive employment trends

Throughout the OECD individuals with a disability have lower employment rates than those without a disability, and health problems often are significant barrier to employment (see Chapter 2). However, there are marked differences in the employment prospects of disabled people both in absolute terms and relative to the non-disabled population. In 2012, 40% of people with a disability had a job in Australia. This compares unfavourably to employment rates of over 45% for example in the United Kingdom and Canada, over 50% in France, Germany and Sweden and 61%

in Switzerland (Figure 1.14). The ratio of employment rates of people with disability over those without disability is around 0.5 in Australia, while it reaches 0.7 or more in Austria, Finland, France, Germany, Sweden and Switzerland. Italy and the Slovak Republic also have small gaps in relative terms, but this must be seen against the background of low employment rates overall.

Figure 1.14. **There is a large gap between employment rates for disabled and non-disabled people everywhere and in Australia especially**

Employment rates of persons (aged 15-64) with and without a disability, 2012

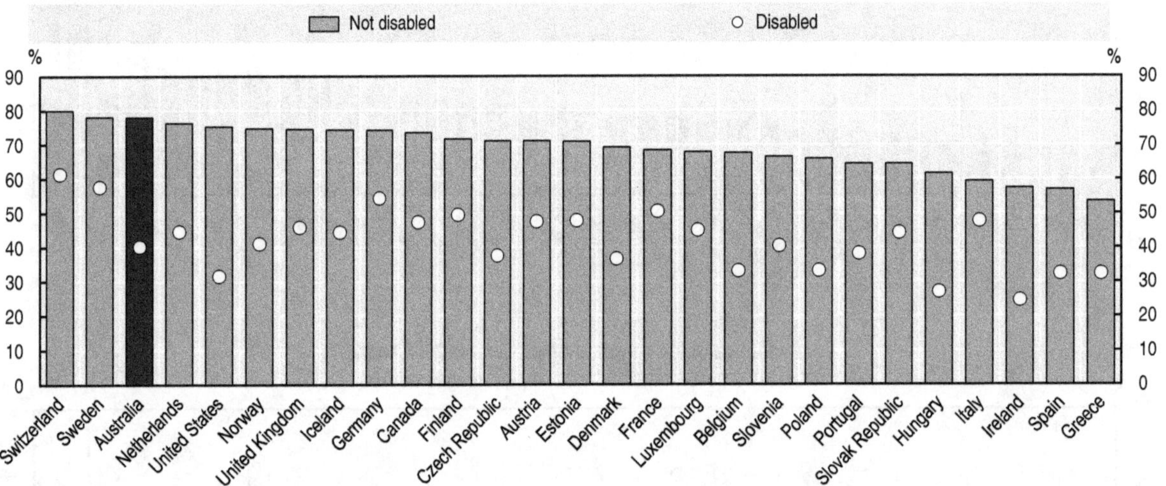

Source: EU-SILC 2012 except: Australia: Survey of Disability and Carers 2012, Australian Bureau of Statistics, 4430.0 – Disability, Ageing and Carers, Australia: Summary of Findings, 2012; Canada: Canadian Survey on Disability, 2012, Statistics Canada. Table 115-0005 – Labour force status for adults with and without disabilities, by sex and age group, Canada, provinces and territories; Norway: LFS 2012 Q2, http://www.ssb.no/en/arbeid-og-lonn/statistikker/akutu; United Kingdom: LFS 2012; United States: Survey of Income and Program Participation, SIPP 2008 Panel, wave 13, September 2012 to December 2012, http://www.census.gov/programs-surveys/sipp/data/2008-panel.html.

StatLink http://dx.doi.org/10.1787/888933447431

Furthermore, disabled people have not benefitted from the positive employment trend in Australia over the last two decades. Already since 1998 the employment rate of people with a disability is deadlocked at around 40% (it was 41.9% in 1998 and 39.8% in 2003; OECD, 2007). In contrast, the employment rate for the working-age population as a whole increased by 4.5 percentage points from 1998 to 2012, leading to a fall in the relative employment rate of disabled people.

Low employment rates of people with disability come with high social costs. Even though most non-employed people with disability receive some public benefits, they have much lower incomes and a much higher poverty risk. In Australia, the United States, Canada, Ireland and Korea people with a disability have a poverty risk double that of people without disability and poverty affects more than 30% of people with disability. On the contrary, in Sweden, Norway, the Slovak Republic and the Netherlands there is little difference in poverty risks between the two population groups (OECD, 2010). Employment in turn is the most important factor in reducing poverty risks and employed disabled people in Australia have poverty rates around 20% below the average for the total working-age population (OECD, 2007).[4]

Like many other OECD countries, Australia has seen disability benefit claim rates rise steadily over the 1990s and early 2000s. The proportion of the population aged 20-64 years receiving disability benefits increased from 3.1% in 1990 to 5.5% in 2002 (OECD, 2007). A series of reforms since 2006 in Australia introduced stricter entitlement criteria for Disability Support Pension, the main disability-related benefit. The reforms resulted in a halt of the rising recipient rates and since 2006 around 5.5% of the population aged 20-64 years receives disability benefits. Disability recipient numbers are expected to grow over the coming decade, mainly driven by population aging (NCOA, 2014). A number of countries through comprehensive disability benefit reform have managed to even reduce disability benefit recipient rates. Most of them, including the United Kingdom, Sweden, Finland, the Netherland and Slovenia, had much higher rates than Australia in 2002 and still have higher recipient rates in 2012 (Figure 1.15). However, these higher rates may partly be explained by the fact that all those countries have contributory based benefits, whereas in Australia all income-replacement benefits are means-tested.

Figure 1.15. **Disability benefit recipient rates have slightly decreased over the past decade in Australia**

Percent of population aged 20-64 receiving disability benefits, 2002 and 2012/13[a]

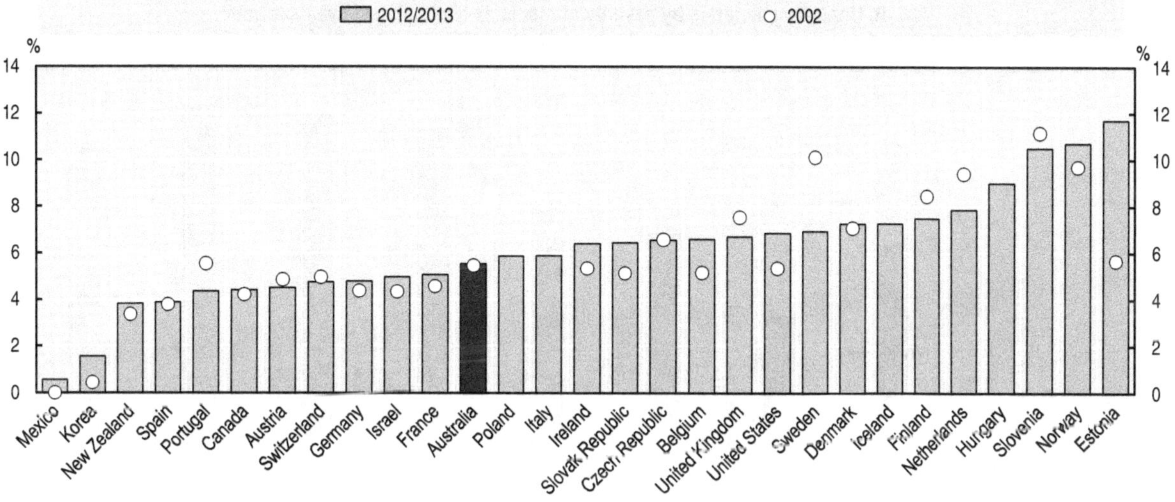

a) Year 2012/13 refers to 2007 for Canada and France, to 2008 for Austria and Korea, to 2010 for Spain and to 2013 for Australia, Czech Republic, Estonia, Finland and the United States.

Source: Updated data from Figure 2.9 of OECD (2010), *Disability and Work: Breaking the Barriers: A Synthesis of Findings across OECD Countries*, OECD Publishing, Paris, http://dx.doi.org/10.1787/9789264088856-en.

StatLink http://dx.doi.org/10.1787/888933447448

People with mental ill-health have poor labour market outcomes

Most people with poor mental health are in work. Even among those with severe mental disorders more than 40% have a job (or more than that in Switzerland). Employment rates for people with mild-to-moderate and severe mental ill-health in Australia are about average in a comparison with ten other OECD countries for which comparable data is available. The employment gap with people with no mental ill-health however is significant: Australia has the largest employment gap for people with severe (34 percentage points) and mild-to-moderate (14 percentage points) mental illness (Figure 1.16, Panel A).

Figure 1.16 **Employment and unemployment gaps are considerable for people with mental health conditions**

A. Employment-population ratio by severity of mental ill-health, latest available year
(employed people as a proportion of the working-age population)

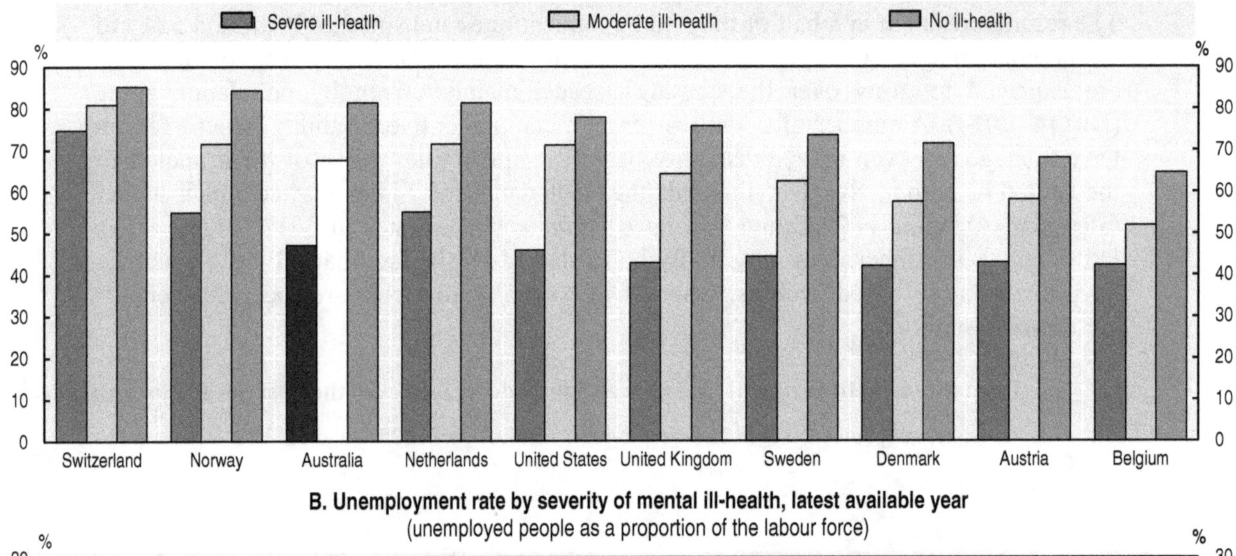

B. Unemployment rate by severity of mental ill-health, latest available year
(unemployed people as a proportion of the labour force)

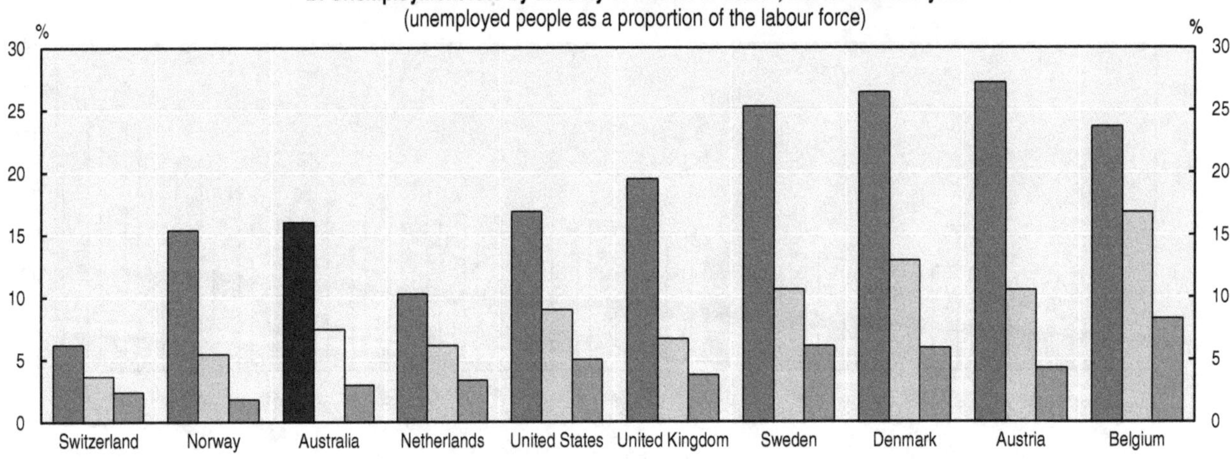

Source: OECD (2015), *Fit Mind, Fit Job: From Evidence to Practice in Mental Health and Work*, Mental Health and Work, OECD Publishing, Paris, http://dx.doi.org/10.1787/9789264228283-en.

StatLink http://dx.doi.org/10.1787/888933447452

Many people who suffer from mental ill-health want to work but cannot find jobs and around a fifth of the Australian population that is out of the labour market reports poor mental health (in comparison to around 10% of the working-age population, see Chapter 2). Across OECD countries for which comparable data is available, people with mild-to-moderate mental illness are twice as likely to be unemployed, while jobless rates among people with severe disorders are, in many countries, four or five times as high as those with no mental health conditions. In Australia the unemployment rate for people with mild-to-moderate mental ill-health is 2.5 times higher than that for people with no mental ill-health, and that of people with severe mental ill-health is more than five times higher (Figure 1.16, Panel B).

Because people with mental health conditions perform so poorly on the labour market, they are a major challenge to Australia's different income support systems. About 26% of people with a severe mental disorder receive a disability benefit, but an even higher share (31%) relies on unemployment, lone-parent, or other allowances. Even among people who suffer from a moderate disorder, 40% depend on an income replacement benefit. The share of beneficiaries with a mental disorder in the total disability caseload has risen in Australia, as in many other OECD countries. By 2013, the primary condition of 31% of all disability benefit claimants was mental ill-health – up from 25% ten years ago (OECD, 2015c).

Labour force participation of Indigenous Australians is low

Aboriginals and Torres Strait Islanders, jointly referred to as Indigenous Australians, represent 2.7% of the total population aged 15-64 years and they have a very low employment rate in comparison to the non-Indigenous population. In 2014/15, only 48.4% of the Indigenous working-age population were in employment, compared to 72.6% of the non-Indigenous population. Indigenous Australians are also more than three times as likely as non-Indigenous people to be unemployed (ABS, 2014).

Together with Australia five other OECD countries, i.e. Canada, Chile, Mexico, New Zealand and the United States also collect data for Indigenous populations. There are marked differences in the size of these populations (aged 15/16 years and above[5]): in the United States Indigenous people represent 1.1% of the population, in Canada 3%, in Chile 8.3%, in Mexico 20.5%, and in New Zealand 12.0% of the population (Annex 1.A1, Table 1.A1.1). In all these countries, the Indigenous population has a lower employment rate. However, there are marked differences in the employment prospects of Indigenous people, and Indigenous Australians compare poorly with other OECD countries both in absolute terms and relative to the non-Indigenous population. Whereas less than half of all Indigenous Australians aged 15 years and above are employed, around half are employed in Chile and Mexico, around 55% in Canada and the United States and 58% in New Zealand. In relative terms – employment rates of Indigenous people over non-Indigenous people – the ratio (for the population aged 15 years or more) is around 0.7 in Australia, but reaches 0.9 in Canada, Mexico, New Zealand and the United States, and there is virtually no difference in Chile (Figure 1.17, Panel A and Annex 1.A1, Table 1.A1.1).

A comparison of the employment prospects of Indigenous Australians by state/territory and population density shows that employment rates are closer to those of non-Indigenous Australians in Tasmania and the Australian Capital Territory and in major cities more generally. In contrast, Indigenous Australians have far worse employment prospects in remote and very remote areas (Annex 1.A1, Table 1.A1.1). While employment rates are still low, much progress has been made over the past two decades during which the Indigenous employment rate increased from 40.5% in 1996 to 48.4% in 2014/15 (Figure 1.17, Panel B), compared to an increase in the employment rate of the working-age population as a whole from 67.7% in 1996 to 72.2% in 2015.

Figure 1.17. **Employment rates of Indigenous Australians are low in comparison to that of Indigenous populations in other OECD countries**

A. Employment rates by Indigenous status (persons aged 15 and over), latest year available[a]

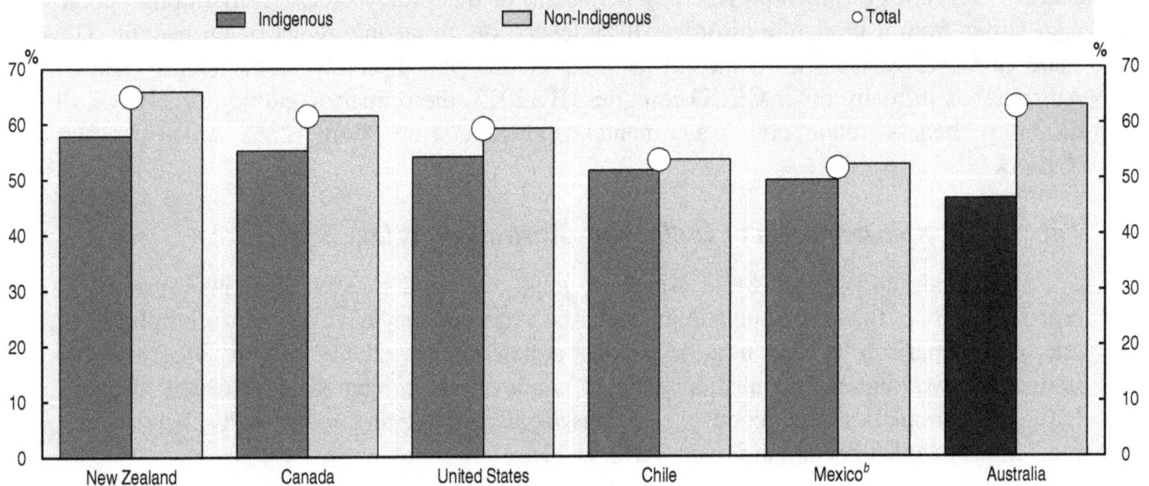

B. Employment rates of Indigenous and non-Indigenous populations in Australia (aged 15 to 64) 1996-2014/15

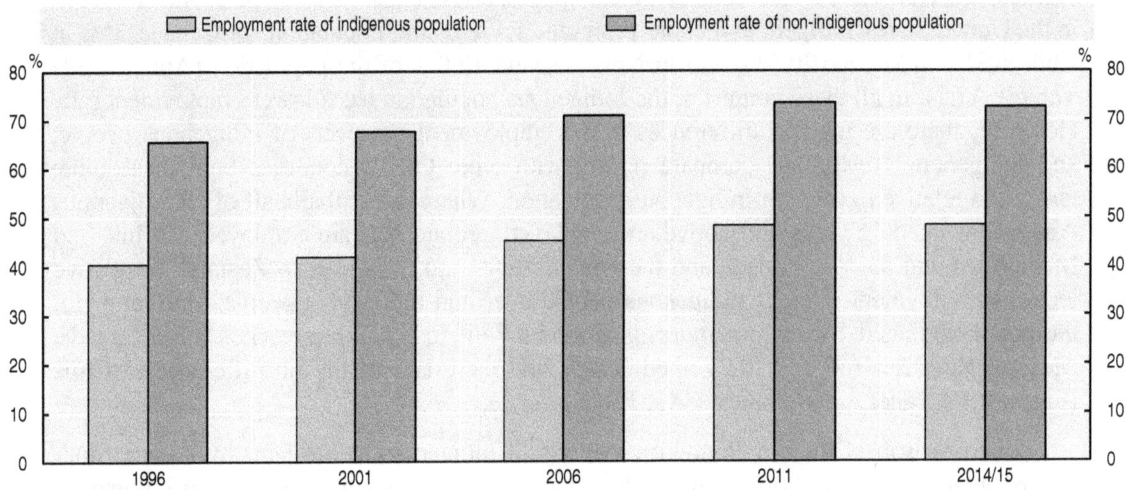

Note: For detailed ethnicities in each country, see Annex 1.A1.

a) Year 2011 for Australia, 2013 for Chile and 2014 for the United States (persons 16 and over).

b) Data are not based on the labour force survey and hence the total employment rate is underestimated by 5.3%. The Indigenous rate does not account for the 5.9% of the population who are speakers of indigenous languages and of which 90.8% recognise themselves as indigenous. This group has a 45% employment rate.

Source: Panel A: OECD calculations based on: Labour Force Characteristics of Aboriginal and Torres Strait Islander Australians, Estimates from the Labour Force Survey, 2011 (Australia); CANSIM Table 282-0227, Statistics Canada (Canada); CASEN (Chile); Database of Intercensal Survey 2015 (Mexico); Household Labour Force Survey table 5, Statistics New Zealand (New Zealand) and BLS Reports No. 1057, November 2015 (United States); Panel B: Population Characteristics Aboriginal and Torres Strait Islander Australians 2001 (ABS), The Health and Welfare of Australia's Aboriginal and Torres Strait Islander Peoples, 2008, Labour Force Characteristics of Aboriginal and Torres Strait Islander Australians, Estimates from the Labour Force Survey, 2011 and National Aboriginal and Torres Strait Islander Social Survey, Australia, 2014–15.

StatLink http://dx.doi.org/10.1787/888933447463

To improve the situation, in December 2007 the Council of Australian Governments (COAG) agreed to a partnership between all levels of government to work with the Indigenous communities. The National Indigenous Reform Agreement set out six "Closing the Gap" targets relating to life expectancy, child mortality rates, education and employment. The employment target is to halve the gap in employment outcomes within a decade, measured through the employment-to-population ratio for the working-age population, the unemployment rate, and the labour force participation rate with 2008 data as baseline (COAG, 2012). Notwithstanding a more positive trend for Indigenous Australians, the employment rate gap was still 24 percentage points in 2014/15 and it is unlikely that an envisaged gap of 12 percentage points by 2018 can be achieved. Some of the difference in labour market outcomes between Indigenous and non-Indigenous Australians is driven by different characteristics of the two populations: Indigenous Australians are on average younger, have lower levels of education, are more likely to have chronic health conditions and report poor health status, and they are more like to live in remote areas. ABS (2014) found educational attainment to be the single most important factor in explaining the employment gap. With the same proportion of people in each education category as non-Indigenous people, the gap in labour force participation of Indigenous Australians would decrease by half. Assuming a similar geographic dispersion and health status in addition would further decrease the gap to less than a third of its current level.[6]

Key findings

Australia's economy has been doing well in the past few decades and this is reflected in high rates of labour force participation and employment. However, significant pockets of non-employment and underemployment exist for particular groups of the population, for a number of reasons, including policies and institutions, often resulting in significant poverty risks for these groups. Policies to increase labour force participation of underrepresented groups would have multiple effects; they would increase wellbeing of these groups and contribute to higher and more inclusive economic growth. The groups most affected include the following:

- Women with young children and in particular lone parents
- Women more generally, including older women
- People with a disability
- People with mental health conditions
- Disadvantaged youth
- Indigenous Australians

Helping these groups better will require addressing their often multiple employment barriers and providing more integrated social, health and employment services.

Notes

1. The Fair Work Act introduced a new provision preventing employers from dismissing a worker on the basis of redundancy without first considering opportunities for redeployment within the company or an associated entity of the company. Moreover, the size threshold for exemption from the main employment protection provisions was reduced from 100 to 15 workers. These changes resulted in an increase of Australia's position on the OECD's indicator on the strictness of employment protection for regular contracts from the third lowest position in 2009 to the eighth lowest position in 2010 (OECD Indicators of Employment Protection, www.oecd.org/employment/emp/oecdindicatorsofemploymentprotection.htm).

2. The analysis based on the Household, Income and Labour Dynamics in Australia (HILDA) survey presented here includes employees aged 20 to 64 years who were retrenched for economic reasons or for cause from their last job. The estimates from the Australian Labour Force Survey (LFS) relate to employees aged 15 to 64 years who were retrenched in any job held in the three months prior to the survey reference week, as well as self-employed individuals whose business closed down for economic reasons.

3. OECD analysis based on Household, Income and Labour Dynamics in Australia (HILDA) survey.

4. A person is defined as living in poverty, if the income of the household is less than 50% of the median income. The figure for Australia refers to the year 2003, when the relative poverty risk of employed people with a disability was 0.81 in comparison to the working-age population as a whole.

5. Data for the United States refers to the population aged 16 years and above. For all other countries the data refers to the population aged 15 years and above. See Annex 1.A1, Table 1.A1.1 for all details.

6. ABS (2014) uses the technique of standardisation to show the effect on labour force participation and unemployment levels of a number of key characteristics including age, education, remoteness and health. These key characteristics were standardised for the Indigenous population to match that of the non-Indigenous population. In addition, multiple standardisations were performed (effectively giving the Indigenous population the same age structure, education outcomes, geographical dispersion or health status as the non-Indigenous population). The multiple standardisations show that the characteristics affect each other. Given this interaction, the difference each characteristic contributes on its own will not add up to the combined difference. Any differences remaining between the two populations after the standardisation will not be due to the differences in that factor (that is, if educational attainment is the same, any remaining difference will not be due to education).

References

ABS – Australian Bureau of Statistics (2016), "Labour Force, Australia, Detailed, Quarterly", August, Catalogue number 6291.0.55.003, http://www.abs.gov.au/browse?opendocument&ref=topBar.

ABS (2014), "Exploring the Gap in Labour Market Outcomes for Aboriginal and Torres Strait Islander Peoples", *Australian Social Trends*, www.abs.gov.au/socialtrends.

ABS (2013), "Forms of Employment, Australia", Australian Bureau of Statistics, Canberra, November, www.abs.gov.au/ausstats/abs@.nsf/mf/6359.0.

Commonwealth of Australia (2015), "2015 Intergenerational Report: Australia in 2055", The Treasury, Canberra, www.treasury.gov.au/PublicationsAndMedia/Publications/2015/2015-Intergenerational-Report.

COAG – Council of Australian Governments (2012), "National Indigenous Reform Aagreement (Closing the Gap)", www.federalfinancialrelations.gov.au/content/national_agreements.aspx.

Department of Employment (2016), "Small Area Labour Markets Australia", June Quarter, Labour Market Research and Analysis Branch, Labour Market Strategy Group.

Kent, C. (2014), "Cyclical and Structural Changes in the Labour Market", Address on Labour Market Developments, hosted by The Wall Street Journal, 16 June, www.rba.gov.au/speeches/2014/sp-ag-160614.html.

NAB – National Australia Bank (2016), "State Update: Northern Territory", July.

NCOA – National Commission of Audit (2014), "Towards Responsible Government – Appendices to the Report of the National Commission of Audit", Volume 1, February, www.ncoa.gov.au/report/index.html.

OECD (2017), *Dare to Share: Germany's Experience Promoting Equal Partnership in Families*, OECD Publishing, Paris, http://dx.doi.org/10.1787/9789264259157-en.

OECD (2016a), *OECD Economic Outlook*, Volume 2016, Issue 1, OECD Publishing, Paris, http://dx.doi.org/10.1787/eco_outlook-v2016-1-en.

OECD (2016b), *Investing in Youth: Australia*, Investing in Youth, OECD Publishing, Paris, http://dx.doi.org/10.1787/9789264257498-en.

OECD (2016c), *Education at a Glance 2016*, OECD Indicators, OECD Publishing, Paris, http://dx.doi.org/10.1787/eag-2016-en.

OECD (2015a), *OECD Skills Outlook 2015: Youth, Skills and Employability*, OECD Publishing, Paris, http://dx.doi.org/10.1787/9789264234178-en.

OECD (2015b), *Fit Mind, Fit Job: From Evidence to Practice in Mental Health and Work*, Mental Health and Work, OECD Publishing, Paris, http://dx.doi.org/10.1787/9789264228283-en.

OECD (2015c), *Mental Health and Work: Australia*, Mental Health and Work, OECD Publishing, Paris, http://dx.doi.org/10.1787/9789264246591-en.

OECD (2014), "Non-regular Employment, Job Security and the Labour Market Divide", in *OECD Employment Outlook 2014*, OECD Publishing, Paris, http://dx.doi.org/10.1787/empl_outlook-2014-7-en.

OECD (2013a), "Protecting Jobs, Enhancing Flexibility: A New Look at Employment Protection Legislation", *OECD Employment Outlook 2013*, OECD Publishing, Paris, http://dx.doi.org/10.1787/empl_outlook-2013-6-en.

OECD (2013b), "Back to Work: Re-employment, Earnings and Skill Use After Job Displacement", Final Report, Directorate for Employment Labour and Social Affairs, OECD Publishing, Paris, October, www.oecd.org/els/emp/Backtowork-report.pdf.

OECD (2012), *Closing the Gender Gap: Act Now*, OECD Publishing, Paris, http://dx.doi.org/10.1787/9789264179370-en.

OECD (2010), *Sickness, Disability and Work: Breaking the Barriers: A Synthesis of Findings across OECD Countries*, OECD Publishing, Paris, http://dx.doi.org/10.1787/9789264088856-en.

OECD (2007), *Sickness, Disability and Work: Breaking the Barriers. Vol. 2: Australia, Luxembourg, Spain and the United Kingdom*, OECD Publishing, Paris, http://dx.doi.org/10.1787/9789264038165-en.

The Australian (2016), "Car Industry Closure Puts Thousands of Jobs at Risk", 16 February.

Database references

OECD Labour Force Statistics Database, LFS by sex and age – indicators, http://stats.oecd.org//Index.aspx?QueryId=54218

OECD Labour Force Statistics Database, Incidence of FTPT employment – national definitions, http://dotstat.oecd.org//Index.aspx?QueryId=9582.

OECD Labour Force Statistics Database, Incidence of unemployment by duration http://stats.oecd.org//Index.aspx?QueryId=9593.

OECD Labour Force Statistics Database, LFS by sex and age – indicators, http://stats.oecd.org//Index.aspx?QueryId=54218.

OECD Regional Statistics Database, Regional Demography, http://stats.oecd.org/Index.aspx?DataSetCode=REGION_DEMOGR.

OECD Short-Term Labour Market Statistics – Employment Rates, http://stats.oecd.org//Index.aspx?QueryId=35253.

OECD Short-Term Labour Market Statistics dataset, Harmonised Unemployment Rates http://stats.oecd.org//Index.aspx?QueryId=36324.

Annex 1.A1

Employment outcomes for indigenous populations

Table 1.A1.1. **Population shares, employment rates and coverage of Indigenous populations in OECD countries**

A. Population shares and employment rates

Country	Age group	Share of indigenous population	Employment rate (total population)	Employment rate of indigenous population	Employment rate of non-indigenous population	Year
Australia	15+	2.0	62.9	46.4	63.2	2011
	15-64	2.3	72.8	48.3	73.4	2011
Australia	15-64	2.7	72.0	48.4	72.6	2014/15
New South Wales		2.6	70.7	53.1	71.2	2014/15
Victoria		0.8	71.4	52.8	71.5	2014/15
Queensland		3.7	73.1	49.6	74.0	2014/15
South Australia		2.1	71.1	46.6	71.6	2014/15
Western Australia		3.1	75.0	39.5	76.1	2014/15
Tasmania		4.7	69.5	54.8	70.2	2014/15
Northern Territory		23.1	72.4	36.8	83.0	2014/15
Australian Capital Territory		1.6	76.4	62.8	76.6	2014/15
Major Cities	15-64			57.5	72.7	2014/15
Inner Regional				48.2	70.6	2014/15
Outer Regional				45.4	74.1	2014/15
Remote regions	15-64			37.0	83.4	2014/15
Remote				40.4	82.5	2014/15
Very remote				35.1	84.7	2014/15
Canada	15+	3.0	61.3	55.2	61.4	2015
	15-64	3.3	72.5	60.3	72.9	2015
Chile	15+	8.3	53.3	51.5	53.4	2013
Mexico	15+	20.5	51.8	49.7	52.5	2015
New Zealand	15+	12.0	64.8	57.8	65.8	2015
United States	16+	1.1	59.0	54.0	59.1	2014

B. Coverage of indigenous populations

Country	Indigenous populations
Australia	Aboriginal and Torres Strait Islanders
Canada	First Nations, Inuit and Métis
Chile	Atacameño (Linkán Antai), Aymara, Coya, Diaguita, Kawésqar (Alacalufes), Mapuche, Quechua, Rapa-Nui (Pascuenses) and Yagán (Yámana)
Mexico	Indigenous population by self-ascription. Not included in the data are those who consider themselves as a "population speaking indigenous languages" accounting for 6.8% of the total population.
New Zealand	Māori
United States	Amercian Indian and Alaska Native

StatLink http://dx.doi.org/10.1787/888933447532

Chapter 2

Multiple barriers to employment: The facets of joblessness in Australia

Australia has a substantial group of out-of-work individuals that could benefit from targeted labour market activation policy interventions. These persistently unemployed or inactive individuals, as well as workers with very low work intensity, are potentially constrained from (fully) participating in the labour market by one or multiple employment barriers. Many of the individuals with no, or weak, labour-market attachment have low levels of employability because of lack of work experience or because of existing care responsibilities or health limitations, while others might lack motivation because of high levels of non-labour income or replacement benefits. Understanding the combination of employment barriers that individuals are facing is crucial for targeting and tailoring successful activation policies. This chapter identifies policy-relevant groups (or "clusters") of individuals with similar combinations of different types of employment barriers.

Introduction

The literature on activation and social policies commonly emphasises targeting and tailoring of policy interventions to individual circumstances as crucial factors for policy success. Yet, relatively little is known about what these individual circumstances look like or how they may translate into employment barriers that policies aim to address. Policy discussions often refer to broader labour market groups, such as young people, mature age workers or lone parents. An implicit assumption is that these groups are useful for describing different sets of employment barriers that may inform policy design and implementation. This may or may not be true; for instance being young is, in and of itself, not an employment barrier. As a result, policy interventions targeted on the basis of characteristics such as age, benefit receipt or family situation alone may be ill-adapted to the needs of jobless individuals and those with precarious employment patterns. Chapter 1 shows that in Australia, albeit its generally well-performing labour market, some groups have no or only a weak labour market attachment. An in-depth inventory of people's employment barriers can contribute to a better match between individual needs and available support, and make associated policy interventions more effective and less costly.

Countries across the OECD frequently seek to account for individual circumstances and labour market difficulties by means of powerful statistical tools that "profile" individual benefit claimants using administrative data. In this respect, Australia is one of the most advanced countries in the OECD and its profiling tool – the Job Seeker Classification Instrument – is a fundamental element of its contracted out employment services (see Box 3.2). However, profiling tools are usually applied to the population registered with employment services and, hence, cover only a subset of the out-of-work population. As a result, profiling tools cannot be used to provide a broader perspective on the employment barriers facing the entire population. This chapter adopts a "birds-eye" approach by considering the employment barriers of all those Australians with no or weak labour market attachment (i.e. the target population). After defining the target population and describing its size and composition, the chapter zooms in on the possible employment barriers facing the target population. Using cluster analysis techniques, common combinations of barriers among the target population are identified, and profiles for the different groups are developed. These profiles provide insights into the specific circumstances of individuals with no or weak labour market attachment, and allow for the development of better-targeted policy interventions.

The Australian population with labour market difficulties

Individuals with labour market difficulties frequently move between non-employment and different states of "precarious" employment. As a result, limiting attention to "snapshots" of non-employed (or underemployed) individuals at a specific point in time, such as those based on labour force surveys, may not capture the true size of the population with labour market difficulties or the need for policy intervention. To provide a more comprehensive view on labour market challenges, the *target population* considered in this chapter therefore includes working-age individuals with potential labour market difficulties because they are *persistently out of work* (either unemployed or inactive for more than 12 consecutive months) as well as individuals whose labour market attachment is *weak*. The latter can include individuals with *unstable jobs* working only sporadically, those on *restricted working hours*, and those with *very low earnings* (e.g., due to working informally or in very low productivity self-employment). Box 2.1 defines the sub-groups of the target population and explains how they are identified using the Household, Income and Labour Dynamics in Australia (HILDA) Survey. The target population is a sub-set of the *reference population*, i.e. all working-age adults excluding full-time students.

Box 2.1. Population groups experiencing potential labour market difficulties (*target population for the analysis*)

Using data from the HILDA survey, the target population is defined as the subset of the reference population that is either persistently out-of-work or weakly attached to the labour market.

- **Persistently out-of-work** (*long-term unemployed* or *inactive*). Individuals reporting no employment activity throughout the *reference period.* The reference period corresponds to 12 consecutive monthly observations in the *financial year* plus one additional observation at the *moment of the interview*.
- **Weak labour market attachment**. Individuals reporting employment activity during the *reference period* who are observed in any of the following situations:
  - **Unstable jobs**: individuals working only a limited number of months throughout the reference period. This is defined as having worked less than 25% of the potential full-time working time throughout the financial year (i.e. no more than three full-time-equivalent months).
  - **Restricted hours**: workers who spent most or all of the reference period working *ten hours or less* a week.[a] Individuals working ten hours or less due to participating in education or training or who give the establishment of a business as reason for working part-time, are excluded as they are unlikely to have unused work capacity.
  - **Near-zero earnings**: individuals reporting some work activity during the financial year but zero or *near-zero* earnings (first percentile of all non-zero monthly earnings). The employment situation of individuals included in this group could signal labour market difficulties such as underpayment or informal activities.

a) Because of limited information on hours worked during the financial year, restricted hours is defined as working ten hours or less at the moment of the interview and working part-time during at least six months of the financial year.

Figure 2.1 shows the evolution of the target population in Australia between HILDA survey years 2001 and 2014 (referring to financial years 2000/01 to 2013/14). Individuals who are persistently out of work due to unemployment or inactivity account for over three-quarters of the target population. The size of the target population decreased from 28.3% in 2001 to 22.5% in 2008. The Global Financial Crisis (GFC) resulted in a small increase in the target population in 2009, but it declined again in 2010 and 2011. Following the commodity price crisis it increased again and stood at 23.4% in 2014. The decline in the target population was driven by a combination of falling inactivity and unemployment as well as a reduction in the number of weakly-attached labour market participants. The more recent increase in the share of the target population can be fully attributed to a rise in the share of the persistently out-of-work group. This is consistent with the decline in the employment rate and the increase in the unemployment rate following the GFC and the commodity price crisis (see Chapter 1).

Figure 2.1. **Population groups with potential labour market difficulties in Australia**

As a percent of the reference population (18-64 years old), 2001-14

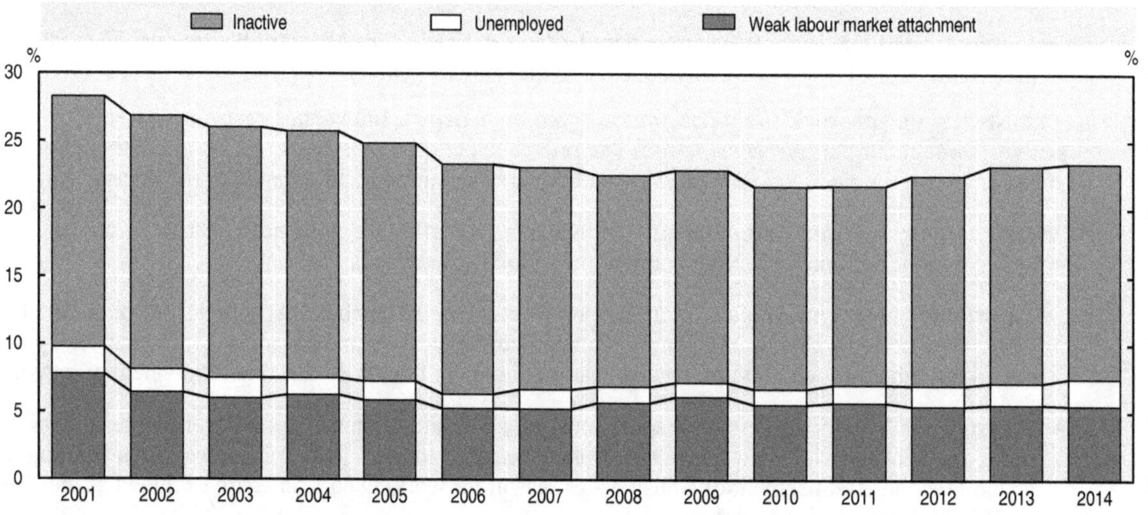

Note: Because of the top-up sample entering the data in 2012, a small break might be observed between 2011 and 2012.

Source: Author's calculations based on HILDA. See Box 2.1 for the definitions of the three groups.

StatLink http://dx.doi.org/10.1787/888933447477

The majority of individuals with "weak labour market attachment" worked part-time throughout the year (11% of the target population), while the rest spent part of the year out of employment (unstable jobs, 9%) or reported working throughout the year but with very little earnings (4.5%). Weak labour market attachment is closely linked to casual employment, with 68% of weakly-attached employees having a casual job (at the moment of the interview). Overall, 13% of all casual workers in the reference population are identified as being part of the target population.

Figure 2.2 provides a more detailed breakdown of the reference population with potential labour market difficulties in 2014. While around 23% had weak labour market attachment, the vast majority was out of work (77%). The most common status among the out-of-work population was inactivity because of domestic tasks (30% of the target population), followed by 16% who reported that they were retired and another 15% who reported that they were unfit to work. Only 8.6% of the target population was unemployed.

Figure 2.2. **Composition of the Australian population with no or weak labour market attachment**

As a percent of the target population, 2014

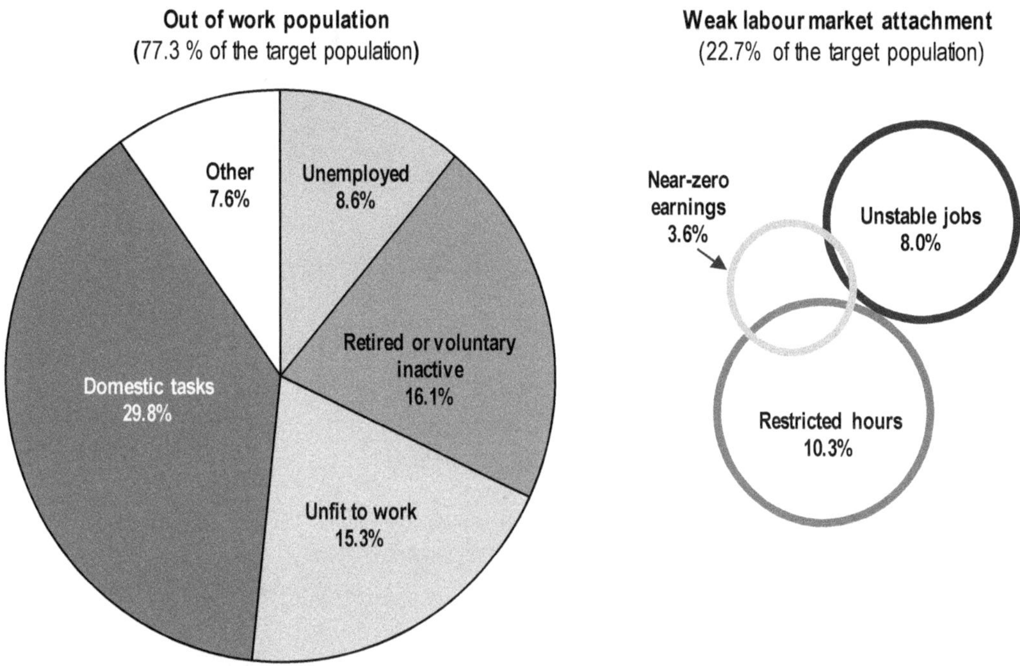

Source: Calculations based on HILDA 2014. See Box 2.1 for the definitions of the groups.

StatLink http://dx.doi.org/10.1787/888933447487

Employment barriers in Australia

Working age individuals with no or weak labour-market attachment may face a number of employment barriers that prevent them from fully engaging in employment activities. In order to make labour markets more inclusive and resilient, a thorough understanding of these barriers is a pre-requisite for designing and implementing policy interventions in a way that is well-targeted and suitably adapted to the circumstances of different policy clients. Following the framework presented in OECD (2015),[1] the analysis presented here examines three types of employment barriers (Figure 2.3):

- Lack of *motivation*: Benefits may reduce the financial incentive to look for a job, e.g. because of low potential pay, relatively generous out-of-work benefits (and potentially missing mutual obligations), or access to high levels of income independent of their own work effort.
- *Employability* barriers: Even motivated jobseekers may struggle to find work due to a lack of skills, limited work experience, care responsibilities and health-related limitations.
- Scarce job *opportunities*: Bringing more people into employment requires addressing demand-side barriers like a shortage of vacancies in the relevant labour market segment, frictions in the labour market due to information asymmetries, or discrimination in the workplace.

Figure 2.3. **Employment barriers: Conceptual framework**

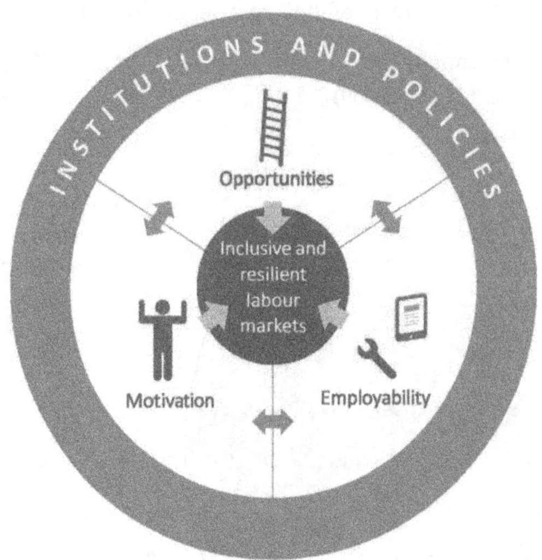

Source: OECD (2015), "Activation Policies for More Inclusive Labour Markets", *OECD Employment Outlook 2015*, OECD Publishing, Paris, http://dx.doi.org/10.1787/empl_outlook-2015-7-en.

StatLink http://dx.doi.org/10.1787/888933447491

Once these different employment barriers – motivation, employability and opportunities – have been identified for the target population, they can be addressed through appropriate social, health and labour market policies and implemented and managed by effective and efficient institutions.

For individuals with potential labour market difficulties the three barriers often closely interact with one another. For example, if there are more job opportunities, it is easier to motivate people to look for jobs or to work on their skills; when jobseekers are motivated, employers will be keener to inform employment services about upcoming vacancies. Thus, motivation promotes opportunities and vice-versa. Identifying these interactions is important for the design of effective and efficient policy interventions, which may often address two or three of the barriers, albeit with varying weights. For example, a direct job creation programme can affect motivation through a "threat" effect, increasing job-finding rates before participation in it has started; it can enhance employability, providing work experience to disadvantaged groups that had limited previous contact with a work environment; and it can offer opportunities, as participants have direct contact with potential employers, and can cite skills acquired on the job when they next apply for a job. Similarly, employment service referrals of jobseekers to vacancies act partly as a motivating factor, intensifying independent job search aimed at finding a job, and partly as an opportunity.

The employment barriers outlined above cannot all be measured directly. To operationalise the concepts, this chapter develops a set of indicators under each of the three categories. Weak motivation is approximated by two indicators for financial work disincentives. The first measures is the income available independently of own work effort, and the second measure is the income gain from own work effort. Employability barriers are conceptualised using measures related to health limitations, care responsibilities, skill levels and lack of experience. Opportunities are measured through the probability of facing a demand-side constraint. Box 2.2 provides more details on the construction of these proxies.

Box 2.2. Measuring employment barriers: Proxies for employability, motivation and opportunities

Using data from the Australian HILDA survey, a set of employment barriers can be defined along the OECD (2015) framework of employability, motivation and opportunities.

Employability

- Skills: Individuals are considered as having a skills-related employment barrier if they have a lower-secondary degree or less (Grade 11 or below) *or* low professional skills.[a] Individuals who demonstrate high skills by having a tertiary degree are assumed not to face this employment barrier even if their most recent job was low-skilled.
- Work experience: Individuals are facing a work experience barrier when they have low total work experience. Low levels of work experience are defined as having spent less than 60% of the potential time in paid work. Potential experience is defined as the total time an individual could have spent in employment, based on the individual's age and taking into account time spent in education. A distinction can be made between people without any work experience and people with "low" work experience.
- Health limitations: Individuals are considered to be facing a health barrier when they report having long-term health limitations, which limit the amount of work they can do, or if they report impairing mental health conditions.[b, c]
- Care responsibilities: Individuals are assumed to have care responsibilities when they have a (minor or adult) family member who requires care and are either *the only* potential care giver in the household, or the only person in the household who is economically inactive or working part-time *because of care responsibilities.*[d]

Motivation

- Non-labour income: Individuals are assumed to face disincentives from working because of high income from other sources than income from labour when their total household income minus the income that depends on the individual's own employment (earnings, earnings-replacement benefits) is higher than 1.55 times the median value in the reference population.
- Earnings-replacement benefits: Individuals are considered having low incentives to work when their earnings-replacement benefits represent at least 50% of their estimated potential earnings in work.

Opportunities

- Demand-side constraints: Individuals are facing a lack of opportunities when their standardised probability of being long-term unemployed (i.e. available for work and actively looking for a job) is larger than one. The probability of long-term unemployment is calculated based on the individual's age, educational attainment, region of residence, gender and migrant status.

For more details, see Fernandez et al. (2016) and Immervoll et al. (2017).

a) Low professional skills refers to individuals who are currently employed as "Cleaners and Laundry Workers", "Construction and Mining Labourers", "Farm, Forestry and Garden Workers", "Food Preparation Assistants" or "Other Labourers", and the unemployed or inactive individuals whose last job was in one of these occupations.

b) Individuals are assumed to have a health limitation when they report having a long-term physical or mental health condition that restricts the amount of work that they can do, and when the degree of this restriction is at least equal to 5 on a scale from 0 to 10.

c) Mental health is measured using the SF-36 Health Survey, an internationally recognised tool for assessing functional health status and well-being. It consists of 36 items measuring eight distinct health concepts. The mental health index ranges from 0 (poor) to 10 (good). Impairing mental health conditions are defined as having a score below or equal to 4.8.

d) Family members assumed to require care are children under the age of 12 receiving less than 30 hours of non-parental childcare a week and adults reporting severe limitations in daily activities due to their health and being economically inactive throughout the reference period (and in the case of those of working age, that "permanent disability" is the reason for their inactivity).

Figure 2.4 shows the share of individuals in the target population and the broader reference population facing each of the employment barriers in Australia. As expected, the incidence of each barrier, with the exception of the high non-labour income barrier, is higher in the target population. The most common barriers include "low" relative work experience (43% of the target population), low skills (38%) and health limitations (35%). The other employment barriers, in particular, "care responsibilities" (20%) and "high levels of non-labour income" (28%), are somewhat less prevalent overall, but may still be very important for some sub-groups. Only a relatively small share of the target population faces "scarce job opportunities" (13%), "high earnings replacement benefits" (9%) or "no past work experience" (7%). The employability barriers are more prevalent for those who were out of work throughout the entire reference period than for those with weak labour-market attachment. The barriers related to motivation, however, are bigger among the weakly-attached labour market participants. A reason for the weakly attached group to have higher non-labour income is that they are more likely to live with a person who is in employment and thus their households have sources of income that are not directly related to their work efforts. Both the out of work and the weakly attached groups have the same probability of having scarce job opportunities.

Figure 2.4. **Type of employment barriers of Australians with no or weak labour market attachment**

As a percent of the target and reference population, 2014

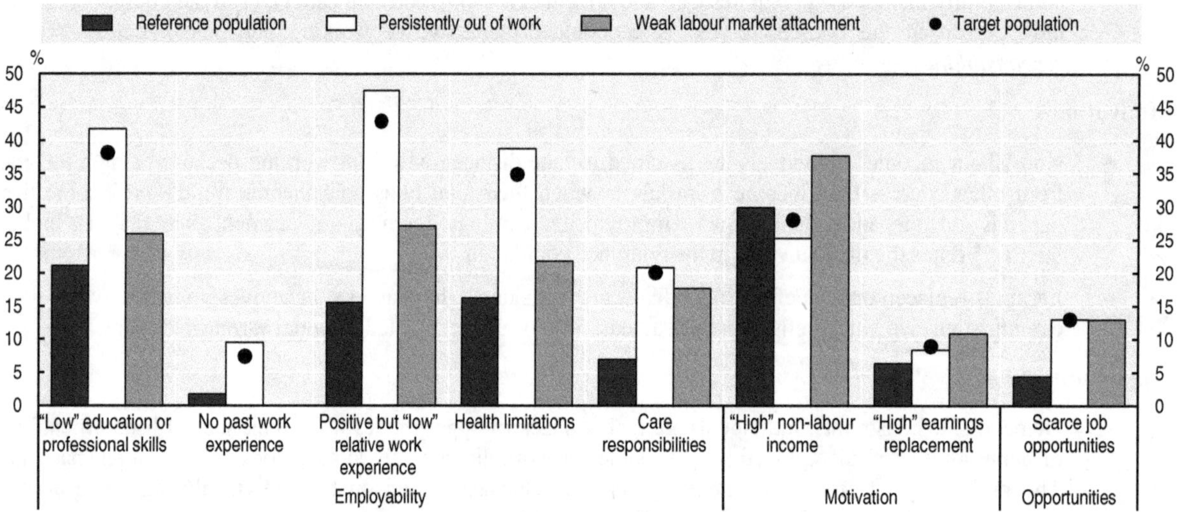

Source: Author's calculations based on HILDA. See Box 2.2 for the definitions of the barriers.

StatLink http://dx.doi.org/10.1787/888933447503

In practice people's individual and family circumstances are complex and often lead to situations where they face multiple barriers to employment. Figure 2.5 shows the number of (simultaneous) barriers faced by individuals in the target population. One third faces two simultaneous barriers, just under a quarter faces three barriers and 8% face four or more barriers. Less than 10% face no major employment barrier. For this group, the employment-barrier indicator may be slightly below the respective thresholds used in this note, or they are not working or are "underemployed" for reasons unrelated to the barriers discussed here – for instance, they may simply have a strong preference for leisure.

Figure 2.5. **Number of simultaneous employment barriers of Australians with no or weak labour market attachment**

As a percent of the target population, 2014

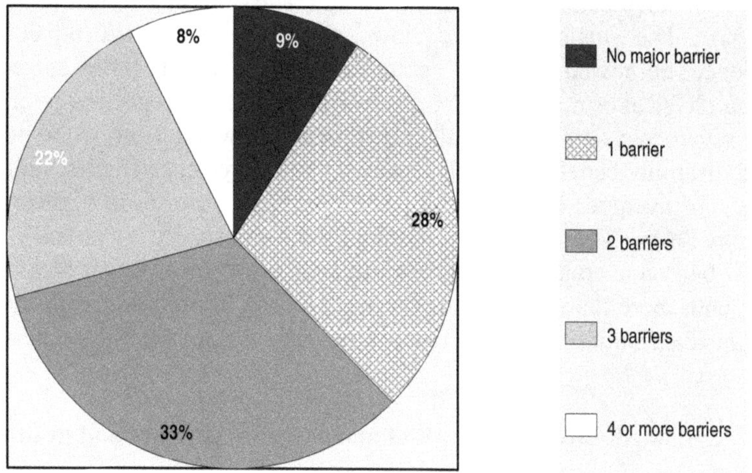

Source: Calculations based on HILDA 2014.

StatLink http://dx.doi.org/10.1787/888933447517

Faces of joblessness in Australia

Using latent class analysis, a statistical method for segmenting, the target population can be divided into groups of individuals facing a similar combination of employment barriers. The goal of the segmenting exercise is to create clusters of individuals that are as similar as possible in terms of their barriers, with the differences between clusters being as large as possible. These clusters will be meaningful for the design, tailoring and targeting of activation and employment support policies, as the success of these policies crucially depends on their ability to address real-world combinations of different labour market obstacles. For more details on the statistical segmentation method, see Fernandez et al. (2016).

Seven different combinations of employment barriers

Using 2014 HILDA data, the segmentation process leads to the identification of *seven clusters* of individuals with no or weak labour market attachment.[2] In the following, each cluster is described in detail (with the clusters sorted by size, starting with the largest): through a Venn diagram to show the extent and degree of overlap of the main barriers characterising the cluster, and a list of selected individual and household characteristics with a "high" probability of occurrence within the cluster. This information can help attach suitable labels ("*faces*") to cluster members. It is important to highlight that the labels are necessarily arbitrary to some extent and cannot substitute for careful examination of the comprehensive list of employment barriers and socio-economic characteristics reported for each cluster in Tables 2.1 and 2.2.

"Low educated women with limited work experience and health limitations"

Cluster 1 represents 25% of the target population and consists largely of prime-age women (68% of members are female, average age 49 years) who are labour-market inactive (94%). The majority have low *education or skills* (66%) and limited work experience compared to their potential (67%). About 58% suffer from some long-standing physical or mental *health limitations*, with 29% reporting poor mental health and 20% a severe physical or mental impediment for work. Forty-four per cent receive sickness and disability benefits and 10% receive unemployment benefits. Individuals in this cluster face an average of 2.2 employment barriers, the third-highest level of all clusters (Figure 2.6). The average equivalised household income is relatively low (AUD 37 040 on average in comparison to an average of AUD 60 664 in the reference population), with more than half of this cluster living in households in the bottom quintile of the income distribution, and the risk of poverty is the second highest (55%) of all clusters.

Cluster 1. **"Low educated women with limited work experience and health limitations"**

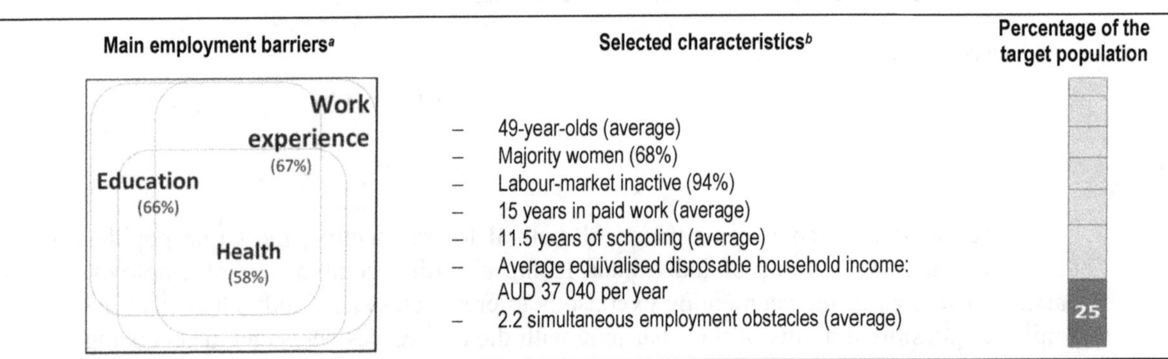

a) Surface areas of shapes in the diagram are proportional to the number of members facing the related barrier ("Proportional Venn Diagrams"). The outer square represents the cluster size (100%). The diagram shows the most prevalent barriers in the cluster and is based on the indicators discussed in Box 2.2.

b) Characteristics that distinguish this group from other groups, i.e. categories that have a high probability of occurring in the cluster. Table 2.2 reports individual and household characteristics in more detail.

Source: Calculations based on HILDA 2014, see Tables 2.1 and 2.2 for full results.

"Experienced early retirees with health limitations"

The second cluster accounts for 20% of the target population, and generally consists of older men (the average age is 56, 75% are aged 55-64 years) with considerable paid work experience (31 years on average, the highest of the seven clusters). More than half suffer from a long-standing physical or mental *health limitation*, and 27% receive sickness and disability benefits and 10% receive unemployment benefits. The majority are labour market inactive (83% during the reference period) with 39% reporting their activity status as "retired" and 21% as "unable to work" because of sickness or disability at the time of the interview. More than one fourth live in households with high levels of income that are not related to their own work effort (e.g. unearned income or the income of a partner), thus weakening their financial *work incentives.* 24% have low *education or professional skills*. Compared to other clusters, individuals in this cluster are less likely to face multiple simultaneous employment barriers (see Figure 2.6).

Cluster 2. **"Experienced early retirees with health limitations"**

Main employment barriers	Selected characteristics	Percentage of the target population
Health (55%) Education (24%) Non-labour incomes (27%)	– 56 years old (average) – Majority men (67%) – Labour-market inactive (83%) – 31 years of paid work (average) – 12.8 years of schooling (average) – Average equivalised disposable household income: AUD 46 618 per year – 1.1 simultaneous employment obstacles (average)	20

Source: Calculations based on HILDA 2014, see Tables 2.1 and 2.2 for full results.

"Mothers with care responsibilities and few other employment obstacles"

The third cluster, which accounts for 13% of the target population, almost entirely consists of prime age (the average age is 34, 95% are aged 25-54) women (96%) with young children who have a partner. These families have on average two children and the average age of the youngest child is two. In the vast majority of cases the partner works (86%), meaning that *care responsibilities* fall on members of this cluster as they receive only little non-parental childcare (the average is 12 hours per week, the lowest of all clusters with children). 84% of individuals in this cluster were labour market inactive throughout the reference period and 75% were still inactive at the moment of the HILDA interview (while 10% were unemployed). Long periods of inactivity also help to explain why over a third (36%) of individuals in this cluster has low overall *work experience* relative to their potential. This happens despite the high education level characterising this cluster, with an average of 14.5 years of schooling (the highest of all clusters) and 68% of members having completed an advanced diploma or a graduate degree. The other common employment barrier characterising this cluster is weak *work incentives* resulting from high levels of household income that are not related to their own work effort (34% of members).

Cluster 3. **"Mothers with care responsibilities and few other employment obstacles"**

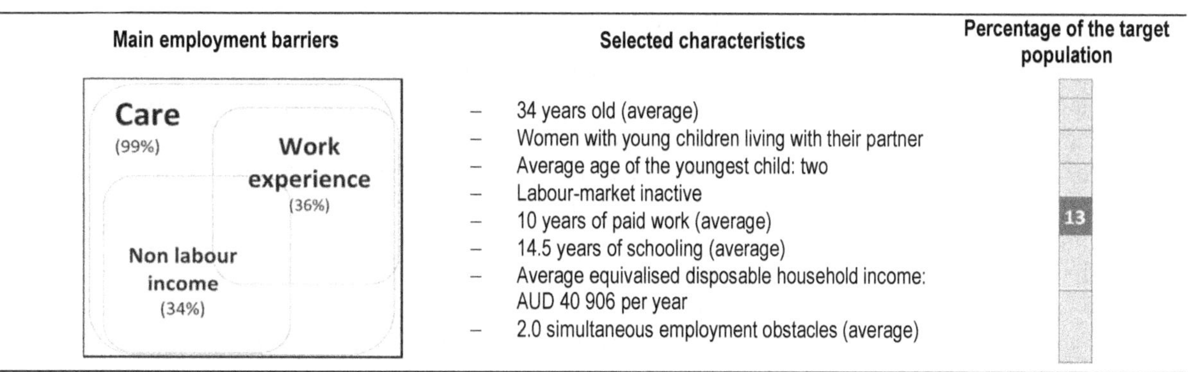

Source: Calculations based on HILDA 2014, see Tables 2.1 and 2.2 for full results.

"Underemployed workers with weak work incentives"

Cluster 4 represents 12% of the target population and it is the only cluster, where the majority of individuals are "underemployment" (83%), as opposed to inactive or unemployed (17%). Individuals in this cluster are also mostly prime age (average age 40) women (66%). About half of the members worked throughout the reference period for ten hours per week or less and another 23% worked for no more than three months during the same period. Another 20% reported work activity throughout the reference period but declared zero or *near zero* earnings; of this 35% were self-employed who mainly declared *zero* earnings throughout the year, while 64% were part-time employees who reported some positive, but low earnings. Only 20% of the part-time employees in this cluster reported being "involuntary part time". Of the others, 53% wanted to work part time (27% because they prefer working part-time, 11% because they like their job, and 15% due to education) while 17% had care responsibilities and 7% a long-standing illness or disability. Many individuals in this cluster face weak financial *incentives to work*: 74% live in households where at least one other person has employment earnings (the second-highest percentage of all clusters) and for 60% of members the level of household income that is not related to own work effort is particularly high (i.e. more than AUD 45 586 per year; Table 2.1).

Cluster 4. **"Underemployed workers with weak work incentives"**

Main employment barriers	Selected characteristics	Percentage of the target population
Non-labour income (60%); Education (20%); Work experience (17%)	– 40 years old (average) – Mostly women – Some work activity during the reference period – 20 years of paid work (average) – 13.4 years of schooling (average) – Average equivalised disposable household income: AUD 54 729 per year – 1.1 simultaneous employment obstacles (average)	12

Source: Calculations based on HILDA 2014, see Tables 2.1 and 2.2 for full results.

"Long term unemployed with limited work experience and low education"

Representing 12% of the target population, Cluster 5 consists largely of younger individuals (average age 31) facing scarce job opportunities (80%): many have been actively seeking employment for more than a year, with an average unemployment spell of 16 months. The majority (57%) were unemployed at the moment of the interview while 40% were labour market inactive. 46% received unemployment benefits during the income reference period. As a result of this long period out of work, the majority (55%) have limited work experience_relative to their potential. Half also have low *education or skills* whereas a significant number (39%) reported a long-standing physical or mental *health limitation* (the average mental health score is the second-lowest of all clusters, with 26% having a score which is lower than 6). Compared to other clusters, individuals in this cluster are more likely to face multiple simultaneous employment barriers (Figure 2.6). The average equivalised household income is the second lowest of the seven clusters and the risk of poverty is high (53%).

Cluster 5. **"Long term unemployed with limited work experience and low education"**

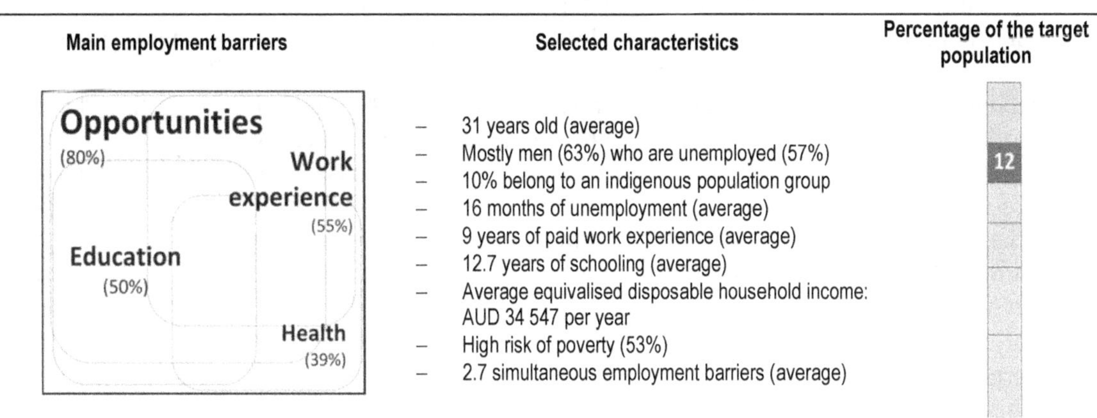

Source: Calculations based on HILDA 2014, see Tables 2.1 and 2.2 for full results.

"Women with limited work experience living in higher-income households"

The sixth cluster accounts for 11% of the target population, mainly consisting of older women (average age 50) who are largely labour market inactive (87%). Although all members have worked in the past with an average of 16 years of paid work experience, for 68% this is low relative to their potential experience. 72% of individuals in this cluster live with someone who is in paid work (their partner in most cases) and many of them (66%) have weak *work incentives* resulting from high levels of household income that are not related to their own work effort (this cluster has the highest equivalised household incomes of all seven groups, AUD 66 680 per year on average). 46% report their activity status as "house work", 21% as "retired" and 16% as inactive due to "other" reasons. About one third has low education or skills. Individuals in this cluster face an average of 1.8 employment barriers (Figure 2.6).

Cluster 6. **"Women with limited work experience living in higher-income households"**

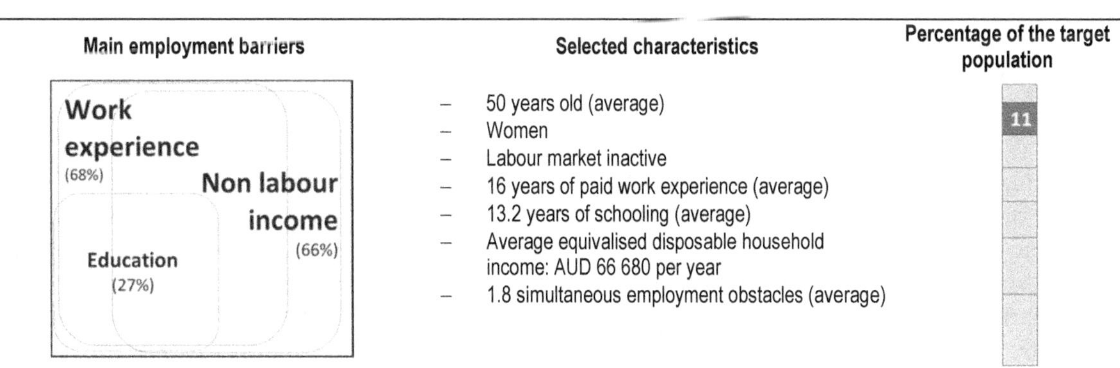

Source: Calculations based on HILDA 2014, see Tables 2.1 and 2.2 for full results.

"Mothers with multiple employment obstacles"

Cluster 7 represents 7% of the target population and consists of younger (33 years on average) women (97%) with children (98%, two children on average). 17% of individuals in this cluster belong to an Indigenous population group. The majority were labour market inactive throughout the reference period (89%), with 71% reporting "house work" as their main activity. 44% live with a partner whereas one third are lone parents. 63% of these women face *care responsibilities* because their children are often of pre-school age (their youngest child is aged 3 on average) and live in households without other *potential* care givers. Although almost all members receive income support in the form of family benefits (95%), 56% are at risk of poverty, the highest proportion of all seven clusters. These benefits are means tested and often weaken the incentives to look for employment and take up work: for 60% of individuals in this cluster the earnings-replacement benefits are high relative to potential earnings in work (Table 2.1). This cluster also has the lowest average number of years of schooling (11.9 years) with 66% having low *education or skills*. One in three suffer from long-standing physical or mental health conditions and for more than one fourth the mental health score is particularly low (less than 6 out of 10). On average, individuals in this cluster are likely to face three or more simultaneous employment barriers (Figure 2.6).

Cluster 7. **"Mothers with multiple employment obstacles"**

Main employment barriers	Selected characteristics	Percentage of the target population
Education (66%) Work experience (70%) Care (63%) Earnings replacements (60%)	– 33 years old (average) – Women with young children – 17% belong to an Indigenous population group – Labour market inactive – 11.9 years of schooling (average) – 6 years of paid work experience (average) – Average equivalised disposable household income: AUD 29 920 per year – At risk of poverty – 3.4 simultaneous employment obstacles (average)	7

Source: Calculations based on HILDA 2014, see Tables 2.1 and 2.2 for full results.

The cluster analysis clearly shows that individuals often face more than one barrier to employment, see Figure 2.6. Only in the "Low educated women with limited work experience and health limitations" and "Underemployed workers with weak work incentives" clusters the majority of individuals face only one barrier. The cluster of "Mothers with multiple employment obstacles" has the highest number of simultaneous barriers, with over three quarters of individuals facing three or more barriers. Details on the prevalence of each barrier per cluster are shown in Table 2.1. Further details for each cluster, such as individual and household characteristics and labour market status, are provided in Table 2.2.

Figure 2.6. **Share of individuals facing multiple employment barriers in each group of individuals with no or weak labour market attachment**

In descending order of shares facing four barriers or more, 2014

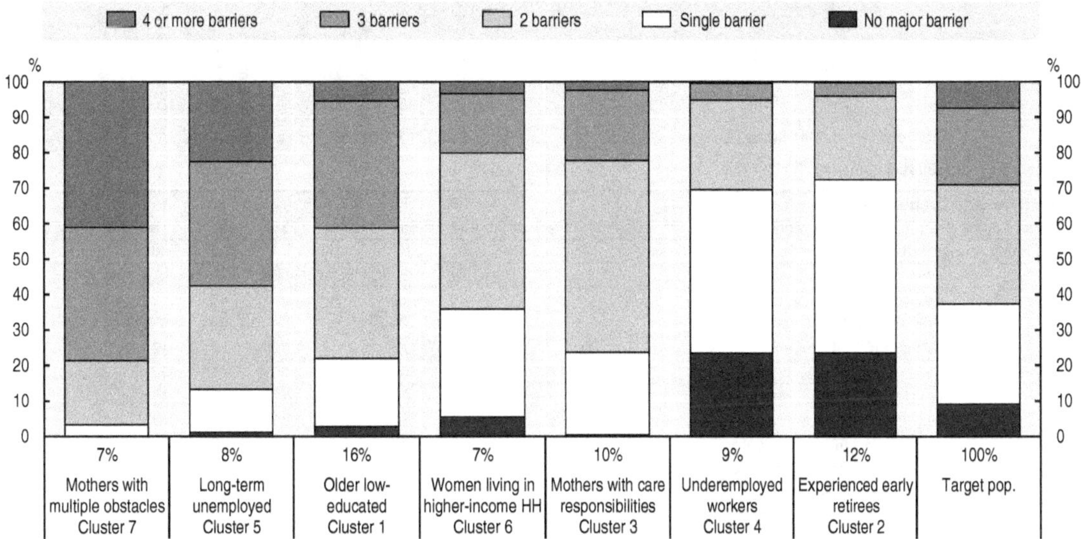

Note: Cluster sizes are reported on the horizontal axis.

Source: Calculations based on HILDA 2014.

StatLink http://dx.doi.org/10.1787/888933447528

Table 2.1. **Core characteristics of groups of individuals with no or weak labour market attachment**

Percentage of individuals with selected characteristics, by cluster (latent class estimates), 2014

	Abbreviated cluster name	Older low-educated	Experienced early retirees	Mothers with care responsibilities	Under- employed workers	Long-term unemployed	Women living in higher-income HH	Mothers with multiple obstacles	Target population	Working age population[a]
	Cluster number	*1*	*2*	*3*	*4*	*5*	*6*	*7*		
	Cluster Size (% of target population)	**25**	**20**	**13**	**12**	**12**	**11**	**7**	**100**	
Core indicators	"Low" education or skills	66	24	9	20	50	27	66	38	21
	No past work experience	6	0	8	17	15	0	18	7	2
	Positive but "low" relative work experience	67	8	36	8	55	68	70	43	16
	Health limitations	58	55	5	10	39	9	34	35	16
	Care responsabilities	8	0	99	0	3	3	63	20	7
	"High" non-labour income	9	27	34	60	12	66	5	28	30
	"High" earnings replacements benefits	6	2	9	2	13	0	60	9	6
	Scarce job opportunities	0	8	2	2	80	0	22	13	4

Note: Box 2.2 describes the indicators and applicable thresholds. Cluster sizes refer to the target population as defined in Box 2.1. Colour shadings identify categories with high (dark blue) and medium (lighter blues) frequencies. Complementary categories (e.g. "high" education) are omitted. Additional information on model selection and model specification is provided in Immervoll et al. (2017).

a) Persons aged 18-64 excluding full-time students.

Source: Authors' calculations based on HILDA, 2014.

StatLink http://dx.doi.org/10.1787/888933447546

Table 2.2. **Detailed characteristics of groups of individuals with no or weak labour market attachment**

Percentage of individuals with selected characteristics († †† denote averages), by cluster, 2014

	Abbreviated cluster name	Older low-educated	Experienced early retirees	Mothers with care responsibilities	Under- employed workers	Long-term unemployed	Women living in higher-income HH	Mothers with multiple obstacles	Target population	Working age population[a]
	Cluster number	*1*	*2*	*3*	*4*	*5*	*6*	*7*		
Cluster Size (% of target population)		**25**	**20**	**13**	**12**	**12**	**11**	**7**	**100**	
Number of individuals (frequency, in thousands)		**697**	**556**	**380**	**336**	**328**	**316**	**192**	**2 805**	13 339
Number of simultaneous barriers††		2.2	1.1	2.0	1.1	2.7	1.8	3.4	1.9	1.0
Women*		68	33	96	66	37	100	97	66	50
Age groups*	Youth (18-24)	0	0	4	24	42	2	24	10	10
	Prime age (25-54)	60	25	95	54	56	56	74	57	70
	Old-age (55-64)	40	75	1	22	2	42	2	33	20
Age††		49	56	34	40	31	50	33	44	42
Education	Lower secondary or less	63	23	8	16	45	25	61	36	20
	Upper secondary	12	12	24	31	26	18	16	18	16
	Cert III / Cert IV / Adv diploma	18	43	33	26	23	32	18	28	34
	Bachelor / Grad diploma / Postgrad / Master	7	21	35	26	6	25	5	18	30
	Years of education (average)	11.5	12.8	14.5	13.4	12.7	13.2	11.9	12.8	13.6
Health	Limitations in work activities (score: 10=max, 0=min)††	4	3	0	1	2	1	1	2	1
	Have "severe" health limitations in work activities	20	15	0	4	7	4	6	11	3
	Good mental health (score: 10=max, 0=min)††	6.1	7.0	7.6	7.4	6.3	7.4	6.4	6.8	7.3
	Have "poor" mental health	29	17	6	10	26	9	27	18	11
Migrant		29	32	43	27	23	39	21	31	31
Indigenous		6	2	3	2	10	2	17	5	3
Household type (members with 15+ years are considered "adults")	Single	27	23	0	14	28	10	0	18	16
	Couple without children	45	55	0	50	36	45	0	38	39
	Couple with children	9	7	83	25	15	31	44	26	29
	Lone parents	2	1	6	2	4	1	33	4	3
	2+ adults with/without children	8	8	3	6	7	6	4	6	6
	Multifamily households	8	7	7	4	11	7	18	8	6
Have children* (less than 15 years)		18	13	100	27	28	38	98	38	37
Number of children† (less than 15 years)		1.8	..	2.1	2	2	2	2.1	2.0	2
Age of the youngest child†		7	..	2	8	6	8	3	4	5
Hours of non-parental childcare†		22	..	12	38	31	32	22	19	32
Household with other working household members		43	44	86	74	53	72	48	57	67
Had any work activity	During the reference period	6	13	27	83	25	15	7	23	82
	During the last two years	22	36	42	87	56	33	25	41	86
	During the last three years	34	51	55	89	69	44	38	52	89
Type of labour market attachment during the reference period	Unstable jobs (≤ 3 months)	..	..	14	23	..	..	..	9	2
	Restricted working hours (≤ 10 hours a week)	..	..	13	48	..	..	..	11	3
	Employees with zero or near-zero earnings	..	..	2	20	..	..	..	4	1
Main reason for restricted working hours	Illness or disability	..	..	..	7	..	..	..	8	5
	Care or family responsabilities	..	..	..	17	..	..	..	30	30
	Education	..	..	..	15	..	..	..	10	8
	involuntary (cannot find FT work)	..	..	..	20	..	..	..	16	14
	Prefer working part time	..	..	..	27	..	..	..	23	25
	Prefer current job	..	..	..	11	..	..	..	10	17
	Other reasons	..	..	..	2	..	..	..	3	2
Main activity during the reference period	Working	3	9	12	61	2	10	2	13	67
	Unemployed	3	8	4	7	47	3	9	10	8
	Inactive	94	83	84	32	51	87	89	77	25
Main activity at the time of the HILDA interview	FT worker	0	2	0	13	0	0	0	2	55
	PT worker	3	8	15	55	3	10	3	13	21
	Unemployed	2	9	10	6	57	2	9	12	4
	Retired	22	39	0	1	2	21	1	16	4
	Unfit to work/disable	32	21	1	4	13	6	4	15	4
	House work	31	12	60	9	6	45	71	30	7
	Other inactive	9	9	15	12	18	16	12	12	5

Table 2.2. **Detailed characteristics of groups of individuals with no or weak labour market attachment** *(cont.)*

Percentage of individuals with selected characteristics († , †† denote averages), by cluster

	Abbreviated cluster name	Older low-educated	Experienced early retirees	Mothers with care responsibilities	Under- employed workers	Long-term unemployed	Women living in higher-income HH	Mothers with multiple obstacles	Target population	Working age population[a]
	Cluster number	*1*	*2*	*3*	*4*	*5*	*6*	*7*		
Cluster Size (% of target population)		**25**	**20**	**13**	**12**	**12**	**11**	**7**	**100**	
Type of employment	Employee	..	..	..	64	..	..	..	64	85
	Self-employed	..	..	..	35	..	..	..	33	14
	Family business	..	..	..	2	..	..	..	3	0
Share of emloyees with "casual" job		..	..	..	68	..	..	..	68	17
Length of unemployment spell (months)†		..	..	..	..	16	..	..	16	12
Years of paid work experience† (average)		15	31	10	20	9	16	6	17	19
Equivalised disposable household income (AUD/year - average)		37 040	46 618	40 946	54 729	34 547	66 680	29 920	44 182	60 664
Position in the income distribution	Bottom quintile	55	29	41	25	53	15	56	40	15
	Second quintile	31	22	33	20	26	20	32	26	19
	Third quintile	5	26	15	18	16	19	9	15	21
	Fourth quintile	5	12	7	17	2	26	3	10	22
	Top quintile	4	10	4	20	3	20	1	9	22
AROPE (eurostat methodology)		55	29	40	25	53	16	56	40	15
Material deprivation (eurostat methodology)		8	2	0	1	8	1	7	4	1
Benefits, recipients and average amounts (AUD/year)	Sickness and disability recipients (%),	44	27	2	10	18	10	11	12	6
	they receive, on average†	17 521	16 885	..	..	..	..	..	9 170	16 030
	Unemployment benefits recipients (%),	10	10	2	10	46	4	9	15	6
	they receive, on average†	..	..	..	..	10 588	..	..	4 854	7 833
	Social Assistance recipients (%),	5	3	1	3	1	4	1	1	1
	they receive, on average†	..	..	..	..	..	..	..	..	11 502
	Family-related benefits recipients (%),	29	21	83	25	18	30	95	33	26
	they receive, on average†	13 868	10 319	10 856	..	..	9 330	22 128	1 364	8 697
Live in rural area*		13	13	10	11	10	10	10	11	10
Area of residence	Major cities	65	67	74	73	70	75	61	69	74
	Inner regional AUS	22	22	15	17	19	17	23	20	17
	Outer regional AUS	12	10	10	9	10	6	14	10	8
	Remote AUS	1	1	1	1	1	2	1	1	1

.. Unavailable because of limited number of observations.

† Average across observations with strictly positive values.

†† Average across all observations.

* The variable enters as an additional indicator in the latent class model. See Immervoll et al. (2017) for details.

Note: Colour shadings identify categories with high (darker) and medium (lighter blues) frequencies. The average number of simultaneous barriers per individual is computed for the core indicators in Table 2.1. Income quintiles refer to the entire population. The ***at-risk-of-poverty rate*** is the share of people with an equivalised disposable income (after social transfer) below 60 % of the national median. ***Material deprivation*** is defined as not being able to afford at least three of the following items: washing machine, telephone, TV, decent and secure home, substantial meal at least once a day, a week's holiday away from home each year, motor vehicle, AUD 500 in savings for an emergency, when it's cold keep at least one room warm. ***Sickness and disability benefits*** include Sickness Allowance or Special Benefits, Disability Support Pension, Disability Pension, and Mobility Allowance. ***Unemployment benefits*** include NewStart Allowance, Youth Allowance, and CDEP. ***Social assistance benefits*** include Service Pension, Wife Pension or Widow Allowance, Partner Allowance, War widow's pension, Abstudy/Austudy, Seniors Supplement, and Bereavement Allowance. ***Family-related benefits*** include Carer payment, Parenting payment, Carer allowance, paid parental leave, Double Orphan pension, Maternity Payment, School Kids Bonus, and Family Tax Benefit.

a) Persons aged 18-64 excluding full-time students.

Source: Authors' calculations based on HILDA 2014.

StatLink http://dx.doi.org/10.1787/888933447555

An initial interpretation of the results

The statistical method used to segment the target population is set to create clusters of individuals that are as similar as possible in terms of their employment barriers. At the same time the differences between the clusters should be as large as possible. Nevertheless, a cluster may still combine different types of individuals that require different types of policy interventions to activate them and at the same time one policy intervention may impact on individuals in different clusters.

Within the Australian target population two clusters of mothers with dependent children were identified (Clusters 3 and 7). Women in the two clusters, however, differ substantially in terms of individual and household characteristics, and as a result also face different barriers. Women in the cluster "*Mothers with care responsibilities and few other employment obstacles (Cluster 3)*" are older, higher educated and more likely to live in a major city than the women in the cluster "*Mothers with multiple employment obstacles (Cluster 7)*" group. Women in the former group are less likely to be lone mothers, more often live in households with other working members, and 34% have access to high non-labour income. As a result, these households have a lower risk of poverty and are on average higher up in the wage distribution. Nevertheless, this does not apply to all women in this cluster. A substantial share of "*Mothers with care responsibilities and few other employment obstacles*" has low work experience as a barrier, without having high non-labour income. Contrary to this group, almost none of the "*Mothers with multiple employment obstacles*" have high non-labour income, but they are much more likely to receive a substantial amount of earnings-replacement benefits. Aside from the care responsibilities and high replacement benefits, they are also hindered from participating in the labour market by low skill levels and low levels of work experience, which is linked to a low educational attainment, as well as their age (around a quarter are at most 24 years old). While childcare related policy interventions are important for both groups, "*Mothers with multiple employment obstacles*" will require additional support measures (e.g. addressing skills and health barriers) to help them overcome their barrier to employment. Chapter 3 discusses both childcare policies for women with young children and special needs of lone parent families.

The cluster analysis also identifies two groups of older women facing substantial barriers to labour market participation (Clusters 1 and 6). Both groups have low work experience, but they differ significantly in terms of other barriers. With almost two-thirds of the individuals in the group of "*Low educated women with limited work experience and health limitations (Cluster 1)*" having no upper-secondary degree, this group is much lower skilled than the group of "*Older women with limited work experience living in higher-income households (Cluster 6)*". Aside from low skills and low work experience, women in the former group also have a high probability of having a physical or mental health limitation. The "*Older women with limited work experience living in higher-income households*", on the other hand, have a very low incidence of physical or mental health conditions. But two-thirds of women in this cluster are restricted from labour market participation by high levels of non-labour income, while this is only the case for 10% of "*Low educated women with limited work experience and health limitations*". This difference in non-labour income is also reflected in the share of households with other working members and the substantially higher risk of poverty for individuals in Cluster 1. Many women in Cluster 1 receive sickness and disability benefits (44%). This signals the need for additional policy measures, which better harness the work capacity of people with a disability as discussed in Chapter 3. In contrast, it is less obvious which policy measures could support the activation of individuals in Cluster 6. An interesting fact is that the older women in Clusters 1 and 6 have some similar employment barriers as the younger women in Clusters 7, respectively 3, apart for the care barrier (Table 2.1). A relatively minor care barrier for the older women is not surprising, as their children are generally older. The care barrier at younger age, however, may well drive the outcomes observed around 15 years later.

The cluster analysis identifies a fifth group of individuals, which is mainly composed of women (66%). In contrast to the four previous groups of women, individuals in the "*Underemployed workers with weak work incentives (Cluster 4)*" group are generally not inactive, but had some work activity during the reference period. Like the "*Older women with limited work experience living in higher-income households*", the group of underemployed individuals are often discouraged from (full) labour market participation by high levels of non-labour earnings. The fact that almost 40% of the part-time workers in the underemployed group report preferences as the main reason for not working full-time is likely to be linked to the high levels of outside earnings. Almost three quarters of the individuals in the group of underemployed live in households with other working persons. The age structure of this group is diverse, with one quarter being less than 25 years old and an additional 22% being 55 or older. About two thirds of employees in the "*Underemployed workers with weak work incentives*" are in casual employment.

Two of the identified groups with labour market difficulties do not consist predominantly of women. The first, "*Experienced early retirees with health limitations (Cluster 2)*", groups older inactive individuals, whose main barrier to labour market participation is health limitations and who are predominantly male (67%). The majority of inactive members report being retired or unfit for work as the reason for their inactivity. A substantial share of group members is receiving sickness and disability benefits. These benefits are, however, not high enough relative to potential earnings to generate a barrier to labour market participation, as for only 2% of individuals in this group high earning-replacement benefits are a barrier (i.e. their earnings-replacement benefits represent at least 50% of their estimated potential earnings in work.). Individuals in this group without a health barrier generally have low skills and/or high non-labour income. The large majority of the group members have high levels of work experience, indicating that their current inactivity status is linked to early exit from the labour market, mainly as a result of health limitations linked to age. Hence, activation policies targeted at mature age workers and individuals with health problems are particularly important for this group.

The second male-dominated group are the "*Long term unemployed with limited work experience and low education (Cluster 5)*", 57% of whom were unemployed at the time of the interview. The main barrier for this group is scarce job opportunities, and many group members also have low skills or low work experience. With over 40% of individuals in this group being younger than 25 years old, this group is relatively young. The individuals from this group are overrepresented at the bottom of the income distribution, and as a result have a high risk of poverty. The unemployed individuals in this group are generally long-term unemployed, with on average an unemployment duration of 16 months. Given the young age profile and low skills or low work experience of this cluster, policies aiming to improve labour market and educational outcomes for disadvantaged youth are especially important (see Chapter 3).

While this chapter is mainly of an analytical nature, it provided some cautious initial thoughts about which polices might be relevant for which cluster. This process should be continued to identify existing policies for all clusters and the potential need for further policies to inform the policy dialogue in Australia. While looking at individuals in a cluster as a whole can be insightful, it is also possible to consider different subgroups within the clusters or consider how different population groups spread across the clusters. One group of special interest in Australia is the Indigenous population and Box 2.3 provides an overview on Indigenous Australians in the target population identified in this chapter.

Box 2.3. **Indigenous Australians are likely to face simultaneous employment barriers**

On average, labour market outcomes of Indigenous Australians are lagging behind those of the Non-Indigenous population (see Chapter 1). This also results in Indigenous Australians being overrepresented among the target population that is either "persistently" out of work or has a "weak" labour-market attachment. While representing 3% of the reference population (i.e. working-age adults excluding full-time students), Indigenous Australians represent 5% of the target population. About 40% of Indigenous Australians of working age are part of the target population. Three quarters of them spread over three of the identified clusters: 30% are in Cluster 1 "Low educated women with limited work experience and health limitations", 23% in Cluster 5 "Long term unemployed with limited work experience and low education" and 22% in Cluster 7 "Mothers with multiple employment obstacles". Individuals in these three clusters are the most likely to have a high number of simultaneous employment barriers (Figure 2.6).

Three common employment barriers are characteristic for these three clusters: i) low education and skills; ii) positive, but low relative work experience; and iii) medium to high prevalence of health limitations. Individuals in Cluster 7 also face substantial care responsibilities – a third of them are lone parent families – and have high relative earnings-replacement benefits (i.e. the benefits represent at least 50% of their estimated potential earnings in work), while four-fifth of individuals in Cluster 5 face scarce job opportunities. While not highlighted separately in the cluster analysis, Indigenous Australians are also more concentrated in remote areas, where labour market opportunities tend to be fewer. Overall the results highlight a need for activation, health and social policies that aim at addressing multiple barriers. However, it is important to highlight that these outcomes are by no means unique to Indigenous Australians and, hence, do not call for measures specifically targeted at Indigenous Australians. Designing effective policies for the clusters more generally should also benefit Indigenous Australians. For Clusters 5 and 7, policies for disadvantaged youth and lone parents, discussed in Chapter 3, are particularly important. An additional challenge may be the effective delivery of social and employment services in areas of low population density. In this respect, the Targeted Initiative for Older Workers in Canada is an interesting example for Australia, as it provides employment support for mature age workers in small, vulnerable communities (see Box 3.5).

Key findings

Activation and social policies are often targeted at broad groups of individuals with potential labour market problems, such as youth, mature age workers or lone mothers. The analysis presented in this chapter shows these groups might be too broad to be meaningful for policy making. Broad groups will generally include individuals who do not face employment barriers, and people within these broad groups might face very different problems. This chapter identifies the Australian working-age population with potential labour market difficulties, be it that they are "persistently" out of work or have "weak" labour market attachment due to unstable jobs, restricted working hours, or very low earnings. Together they are referred to as the potential "target population" for activation policies and in Australia they represent 23% of working-age adults (excluding full-time students). A wide range of labour supply factors (i.e. personal and household characteristics) and labour demand factors (i.e. scarcity of labour market opportunities) may act as employment barriers for this population. Individuals in the target population typically face one or a number of such employment barriers that prevent them from fully engaging in employment activities.

The innovative contribution of this chapter is the application of a statistical segmentation method, which divides the target population into groups of individuals or clusters facing a similar combination of employment barriers. For Australia, this segmentation process leads to the identification of seven distinct clusters of individuals with no or weak labour market attachment: 1) "Low educated women with limited work experience and health limitations"; 2) "Experienced early retirees with health limitations"; 3) "Mothers with care responsibilities and few other employment obstacles"; 4) "Underemployed workers with weak work incentives"; 5) "Long-term unemployed with limited work experience and low education"; 6) "Women with limited work experience living in higher-income household"; and 7) "Mothers with multiple employment obstacles". The results in this chapter can be used to inform the policy dialogue in Australia and to identify, for all or selected clusters, the potential need for additional activation policies.

Notes

1. The framework builds on an earlier framework first presented in Immervoll and Scarpetta (2012) and adds institutions as the foundation to this framework.
2. Immervoll et al. (2017) outlines the segmentation method and the process that lead to the identification of the seven groups. Fernandez et al. (2016) describes in detail the econometric model and the related methodological framework.

References

Fernandez, R. et al. (2016), "Faces of Joblessness: Characterising Employment Barriers to Inform Policy", *OECD Social, Employment and Migration Working Papers*, No. 192, OECD Publishing, Paris, http://dx.doi.org/10.1787/5jlwvz47xptj-en.

Immervoll, H. and S. Scarpetta (2012), "Activation and Employment Support Policies in OECD Countries: An Overview of Current Approaches", *IZA Journal of Labor Policy*, Vol. 1, No. 1, pp. 1-20.

Immervoll, H., D. Pacifico and M. Vandeweyer (2017), "Faces of Joblessness in Australia: Using endogenous thresholds to determine employment barriers", *OECD Social, Employment and Migration Working Paper*, forthcoming.

OECD (2015), "Activation Policies for More Inclusive Labour Markets", *OECD Employment Outlook 2015*, OECD Publishing, Paris, http://dx.doi.org/10.1787/empl_outlook-2015-7-en.

Chapter 3

Better mobilising Australia's underutilised labour resources

This chapter builds on recent work of OECD's Directorate of Employment, Labour and Social Affairs, especially a number of labour market and social policy reviews, and proposes options for improving Australia's current activation and labour market policies and for the development of new ones. While briefly describing the Australian situation, the chapter mainly provides examples of good practice from other OECD countries which could inform the policy process in Australia and help to increase labour market participation of underrepresented groups.

Introduction

There is significant unmet activation potential in Australia's labour market and activating those currently outside the labour market or increasing the participation of those with a weak labour market attachment could have widespread benefits for Australia's economy and society. Higher workforce participation can reduce the pressures on the government budget and serve social inclusion and equity goals. This chapter first reviews key considerations that should be taken into account when planning future public investments aimed to increase labour market participation. Building on a series of recent labour market and activation policy reviews of Australia and other countries, it will then consider Australia's existing activation policies and provide a range of good-practice examples from other countries, which could support the advancement of these policies. Not all groups outside the labour market are within easy reach of employment and related services. Therefore, the last section will review population groups with an unmet activation potential, which could be reached for example through better identification or through providing additional supports and services. Again, a number of examples from other countries are presented which could inform the policy process in Australia.

An investment approach to labour force participation

Across OECD countries, employment services and active labour market programmes (ALMPs) represent a substantial expenditure for governments, with active spending ranging from 0.01% to 1.91% of GDP in 2014 (*OECD Database on Labour Market Programmes*). Therefore, rigorous evaluation is crucial to ensure effective and efficient use of public resources in the labour market activation of underrepresented groups. Expenditure in areas such as health or childcare may often be driven by considerations other than labour market participation, but such spending may play an equally important role in supporting labour market participation of these groups. Public spending on childcare is a prominent example as this is driven by considerations of child well-being but has a huge impact on maternal employment. When considering policy options to better mobilise Australia's labour resources it may be important to evaluate government policies beyond existing target groups and also consider the impact of different departmental portfolios. Better co-ordinated and integrated health, social and employment intervention is often the key to activating currently underrepresented groups.

The Australian Budgets of 2015-16 and 2016-17 included the allocation of funding for measures to support a *Priority Investment Approach to Welfare*, to ensure the effective and efficient spending of public resources. While this section argues that the planned actuarial valuation of welfare may be too narrow to ensure an efficient resource allocation, the new *Try, Test and Learn Fund* is a promising step towards testing the effectiveness of innovative policies to increase labour market participation.

Inspired by New Zealand's recent introduction of the "Investment Approach" to welfare, which is designed to reduce long-term reliance on income support, the Reference Group on Welfare Reform (2015) recommended Australia should adopt something similar. The New Zealand investment approach focuses on allocating active labour market resources on those income support recipients where net inter-temporal fiscal savings in the welfare area are the greatest. This actuarial approach predicts the likely long-term welfare expenditure for an individual based on what has happened in the past to welfare recipients with similar backgrounds and circumstances, and targets resources to those groups with the highest estimated welfare cost. Following the recommendation of the Reference Group on Welfare Reform, Australia's 2015-16 budget allocated funds "over four years to develop a detailed annual actuarial valuation of the lifetime liability of Australia's welfare system from 2015, including identifying groups of people most at risk of welfare dependency and the factors that lead to long-term dependency" (The Treasury, 2015a).

There has been some criticism of New Zealand's investment approach (for example in Chapple, 2013; OECD, 2017), as it does not take into account a person's social and economic well-being after moving off benefits; does not evaluate the employment or earnings outcomes of former welfare beneficiaries; and ignores wider benefits such as personal and family well-being (e.g. health outcomes, child well-being) or the impact on local communities (e.g. crime rates). Also, the New Zealand investment approach narrowly focusses on welfare recipients. Other groups which are underrepresented in the labour market (e.g. potential second earners) or those not entitled to income support (e.g. retrenched workers who do not meet the income test), are left aside.

The Australian Priority Investment Approach covers the entire Australian resident population, including both welfare recipients and those not currently in the welfare system. The actuarial model, at this stage of development, focuses on welfare costs only but in developing potential policy intervention, Australia aims to also consider broader costs and benefits beyond the scope of the model. The Baseline Valuation Report acknowledges that the actuarial model is quite financially-focussed and the need to consider not just the information generated by the valuation model, but also short-term impacts over the budget forecast period, wider costs and benefits to other parts of the system and qualitative impacts on people's lives and their lifetime wellbeing (PricewaterhouseCoopers, 2016).

A broader social cost-benefit analysis (CBA) that measures economic efficiency, taking wider costs and benefits into account, would be beneficial. A focus on economic rather than accounting concepts of costs, coupled with an explicit cost-benefit approach to employment support, is likely to yield a more efficient resource allocation – an argument that has also been put forward by the New Zealand Productivity Commission (2016). In its report on more effective social services it recommended *i)* reflecting the wider costs and benefits of interventions; *ii)* addressing the risks of excluding some clients from receiving any service; *iii)* ensuring the model is open and subject to independent actuarial and economic scrutiny; and *iv)* extending the approach to operate at cross-agency and cross-programme level. A recent report on employment assistance by the New Zealand Ministry of Social Development (2016) acknowledges this gap to some extent and proposes to introduce a second measure of cost-effectiveness, the Social Return on Investment, to take a wider view of the costs and benefits of employment interventions.

CBA can be used *ex-ante*, to support government decisions on adopting a new policy or programme, or continuing, expanding or changing programmes or projects, and *ex-post* in a retrospective analysis of a policy, programme or project to evaluate its impacts, demonstrate accountability and justify government expenditure in the next cycle. Standard guidance to support such evidence-based policy making exists, for example, in the United Kingdom through the so-called *Green Book* (HMT, 2011) and in New Zealand through the *Guide to Social Cost Benefit Analysis* (New Zealand Treasury, 2015). An example for an *ex-ante* CBA to assess long-run investments in increasing the labour market participation of an underrepresented group is provided in Box 3.1. This CBA assesses the long-term impact of a potential introduction of universal provision of subsidised full-time childcare for lone parents with children up to 13 years in Germany. The example shows that an overall net government benefit is being achieved only after 20 years.

Box 3.1. Cost-benefit analysis of an introduction of full-time childcare for children of lone parents in Germany

Two-fifth of the around 8 million families with underage children in Germany is headed by a lone parent. While more than two-thirds of lone parents are in employment, lone parent families are more likely to be in poverty than couple families. As formal childcare does not only allow lone parents to participate (more fully) in the labour market, but also offers potential benefits for their children, the German Federal Ministry for Family Affairs, Senior Citizens, Women and Youth commissioned a study to assess the costs and benefits of expanding subsidised full-time childcare and after-school care for lone parents with children up to 13 years.

While universal subsidised kindergarten is available for children aged three and until they enter primary school, the majority of places are half-day only (with huge regional variation in the availability of full-time places). Subsidised childcare for children aged 1-3 years is in the process of being rolled out (see Box 3.10) but again, the availability of full-time places is not guaranteed. Also the majority of German primary schools are half-day only. The study is based on the assumption that universal full-time childcare for lone parents with children up to 13 years is being created (one-off costs, e.g. for building facilities, are ignored), with lone parents incurring around 11% of the gross operating costs for pre-primary care. Schools offering after-school services are assumed to be free for lone parents, although some public schools charge for these services.

Assessing cost and benefits of the introduction of this measure at a 100% take-up rate, the study found:

- For **children of lone parents**: positive impacts on their health and social development and a higher educational attainment.
- For **lone parents**: an increase in employment rates, with the largest increase for those with children under age three; an increase in the likelihood of full-time employment; and a reduction of the poverty risk.
- For **government**: higher public spending due to the provision of full-time childcare, but lower welfare payments; higher revenues due to increased tax revenues and social security contributions, which are projected to increase in the longer run due to increases in lone parents' productivity; and lower expenditure on other services for children and youth (e.g. second-chance education programmes). While the measure results in a yearly government cost in the first 11 years, a yearly government benefit would be realised thereafter, accumulating to an overall net government gain after about 20 years. The rate of return would be around 2.5% after 25 years, 5% after 30 years and increases to about 8% in the long run.
- An increase of the **gross domestic product (GDP) growth rate** by 0.006 and 0.018 percentage points after 20 and 40 years, respectively.

Source: Anger, C. et al. (2012), "Gesamtwirtschaftliche Effekte einer Ganztagsbetreuung von Kindern von Alleinerziehenden [Macroeconomic effects of full-day care for children of lone parents]", Cologne Institute for Economic Research, Berlin; Federal Statistical Office of Germany (2010), "Alleinerziehende in Deutschland: Ergebnisse des Mikrozensus 2009 [Lone parents in Germany: results of the micro census 2009]", Supplementary material for the press conference on 29 July, Wiesbaden, www.destatis.de/DE/Publikationen/Thematisch/Bevoelkerung/HaushalteMikrozensus/Alleinerziehende.html; and Federal Statistical Office of Germany (2016), "Bevölkerung und Erwerbstätigkeit, Haushalte und Familien: Ergebnisse des Mikrozensus, 2015 [Population and employment, households and families: results of the microcensus, 2015]", Wiesbaden, www.destatis.de/GPStatistik/receive/DESerie_serie_00000209.

Across the OECD, systematic evaluation of major policies and programmes to inform future policy making is carried out much too seldom. Whilst Australia has a relatively stronger culture of evaluation with programme evaluation built into new employment policy proposals, a more timely and extensive release of evaluation reports and outcomes is recommended for all Commonwealth-funded programmes in a systematic manner. This could be achieved through devoting a certain share of spending on labour market policies and programmes to their evaluation, using pilots or trials to be able to judge which interventions should be maintained, extended or abolished. Something similar was done in the course of labour market reforms in Germany where evaluation of all programmes is fixed in legislation. A step in this direction in Australia is the allocation of nearly AUD 100 million in the budget 2016-17 over the next four years to the new Try, Test and Learn Fund to "test the effectiveness of innovative policies aimed at reducing long-term welfare dependency" (The Treasury, 2016). With these monies being directed at welfare recipients, they may support improvements to existing labour market activation policies, the focus of the next section in this chapter; however, such funding is unlikely to support policy development for increasing labour force participation more generally.

Getting the balance right: Improvements to existing activation policies

Unlike most other OECD countries, all income-replacement benefits in Australia are tax-financed assistance payments. Australia is also the only OECD country to provide fully privatised employment services. Activation policies are well developed in Australia and generally quite effective in connecting people with jobs and, thereby, contributing to low rates of unemployment. However, there are a few areas in Australia's benefit system and in its approach to activation which could be changed to improve labour market outcomes for a number of groups. This section makes suggestions for possible changes to Australia's contracted-out employment services more generally; discusses aligning mutual obligations for mature age jobseekers with those for younger jobseekers; and addresses activation policies for lone parents and for people with a disability.

Improving long-term employment outcomes for jobseekers

While most OECD countries have an unemployment insurance scheme which provides benefits linked to previous earnings, Australia has an unemployment assistance programme only, which is intended to meet minimum income requirements. As in many OECD countries, unemployed persons receiving public income support are subject to a strict activity test. Benefit recipients must be actively seeking suitable work or undertaking activity to improve their employment prospects. They also must be available for and willing to accept suitable work, including part-time and casual employment, and attend all scheduled interviews with *Centrelink*, the benefit administration agency, and with their employment service provider. While Centrelink is a publicly managed agency, employment services to jobseekers are provided exclusively by a mix of for-profit and not-for-profit private providers contracted by the Commonwealth Government through a system called *jobactive* (Box 3.2).

The provider fee structure changed in a number of ways in *jobactive* in comparison to its predecessor, *Jobs Services Australia.* As discussed in Chapter 1, labour demand and labour supply factors drive regional labour market outcomes in Australia. Fluctuations in regional labour demand due to commodity price movements, for example, are difficult to influence. Policy measures addressing this divergence and supporting the flexibility of labour supply are important and two new measures in jobactive are worth mentioning: *i)* employment service providers supporting jobseekers in *weaker* regional labour markets receive higher fees to reflect the additional costs associated with helping them find jobs in these locations; and *ii)* jobseekers who have been unemployed *for 12 months* can receive a relocation assistance payment to assist them in taking up a job in a more thriving area.

Another shift in jobactive in comparison to Jobs Services Australia is an increased focus on getting jobseekers into a job as quickly as possible. Also short-term jobs of four weeks (e.g. seasonal work, such as fruit picking) are rewarded through the first outcome payment already being available after four weeks (of which providers can claim up to four per year and jobseeker). The rationale is that short-term jobs can provide jobseekers with work experience and work habits, which will be useful for finding longer-term employment (Department of Employment, 2014a). Otherwise, the Australian system is quite exceptional as it reimburses providers for outcomes, not inputs. This feature has been acknowledged in many OECD reports which, however, also conclude that the fee structure could be tilted towards longer-term outcomes to ensure job retention. With the total potential provider fees being available after 26 weeks of employment, longer-term employment outcomes are not sufficiently rewarded in *jobactive*. Paying for employment outcomes beyond 26 weeks could promote employment retention and advancement by rewarding placement into better and more stable jobs and the delivery of pre-placement training and post-placement assistance (see e.g. OECD, 2012a).

Box 3.2. Snapshot of Australia's system of contracted out employment services

Australia is the only OECD country to provide fully privatised employment services. The process started in 1994, with the privatisation of employment counselling for the long-term unemployed. In 1998, Australia fully privatised its employment services replacing the Commonwealth Employment Service. Since then, employment services have been provided exclusively by a mix of for-profit and not-for-profit private providers contracted by the Commonwealth Government over successive three-year periods until June 2015 and a five-year period since July 2015. Initially called the *Job Network*, the system has evolved over time, being replaced by *Jobs Services Australia* in 2009, which in turn was replaced by *jobactive* in July 2015.

Providers are chosen through a competitive tendering process and evaluated through the Star rating system, which ranks providers according to their performance in terms of short-term employment and educational outcomes of jobseekers. Regression techniques are used to estimate the differences between actual employment outcomes and the outcomes that would be predicted based on jobseekers' characteristics. Providers are remunerated through a mix of different fees, which depend on the *service stream* jobseekers are assigned to, age (administration fee only), length of unemployment (outcome fees) and region. For each client they receive an up-front administration fee and an allocation towards their Employment Fund. Allocations to the Employment Fund are made for each individual jobseeker, but they are not attached to a given jobseeker and can be spent on other jobseekers according to providers' judgment on where the money is most usefully spent to enhance employability. Providers also receive a service fee to deliver the programme *Work for the Dole*, where jobseekers undertake six months of a Work for the Dole Activity (15 hours per week or 25 hours for those under 30 years) with a not-for-profit organisation. If a jobseeker is placed into employment, outcome fees can be claimed at 4, 12 and 26 weeks of employment. Of the potential total fees a provider can obtain, the largest amount is outcome fees.

Assignments of jobseekers to the three different service streams – A ("work read"), B ("vocational issues"), and C ("serious non-vocational issues") – depend on the outcome of the Job Seeker Classification Instrument (JSCI). The JSCI is a regression-based profiling instrument that assesses a jobseeker's relative level of difficulty in getting a job in the relevant labour market and likelihood of becoming or remaining long-term unemployed. The JSCI is implemented by the benefit administration agency *Centrelink*, which collects the necessary JSCI information through a questionnaire addressed to the jobseeker and existing administrative records. There are 18 factors characterising an individual included in the JSCI, among them are age and gender, work and jobseeker history, educational attainment, English proficiency, Indigenous status, access to transport, and disability and medical conditions. The JSCI outcome is used to determine the jobseeker's assignment to stream A or B and indicates whether a jobseeker has multiple and complex issues for employment that may require further assessment. Jobseekers that require further assessment are referred for an Employment Services Assessment (ESAt). An ESAt provides a comprehensive work capacity assessment for people with disability or other complex or multiple issues affecting their capacity to work. The ESAt will determine if the jobseeker requires stream C services or referral to other services such as Disability Employment Services (DES).

Source: Department of Employment (2014), "Request for Tender – For Employment Services 2015-2020", Australian Government, https://docs.employment.gov.au/documents/request-tender-employment-services-2015-2020 and OECD (2016), *Back to Work: Australia: Improving the Re-employment Prospects of Displaced Workers*, Back to Work, OECD Publishing, Paris, http://dx.doi.org/10.1787/9789264253476-en.

Longer-term outcome payments could, however, also result in rewarding providers for outcomes that may have been achieved in the absence of a financial incentive. More research is needed to settle this issue. Australia could use the *Try, Test and Learn Fund* (see above) to pilot variations to its existing jobactive payment model to encourage providers to achieve better employment retention.

Longer-term post-placement assistance together with financial incentives was used in the UK Employment Retention and Advancement (ERA) demonstration. The evidence from ERA has influenced the payment model of the UK *Work Programme*, which offers contracted out employment services for the long-term unemployed. Outcome payments for providers are still available for 1.25 up to 2.25 years after the initial placement for providers who achieve employment retention for their assigned programme participants. Provider surveys indicate that Work Programme providers assisted participants with in-work help and advice, but did not pay participants retention fees which were, however, a fundamental element of ERA (Box 3.3). A full impact evaluation is not available to date.

Box 3.3. Promoting employment retention and advancement in the United Kingdom

The UK Employment Retention and Advancement Demonstration

The United Kingdom's Employment Retention and Advancement (ERA) demonstration was a large-scale randomised control trial (over 16 000 people were randomly assigned), which ran from 2003 to 2007 as a pilot programme in 6 out of 37 Public Employment Service (PES) districts in Great Britain. ERA used a combination of job coaching and financial incentives in attempting to help long-term unemployed men and low-income lone parents sustain employment and progress in work after they started working. ERA participants were eligible for a range of additional supports (in comparison to regular PES customers in the control group) over a 33 months service period:

- ERA participants developed an advancement action plan together with specially trained employment advisers, which set out steps to be taken for the individual to find and retain work, as well as advance in employment. Meetings between participants and their ERA advisers were to be held every 17 weeks.
- ERA participants who worked full time for 13 weeks during a 17-week period were eligible for retention and advancement bonuses. Bonus payments were made at meetings between individuals and their advisers.
- ERA participants also were eligible for an hourly training bonus, which they received for work-related training courses completed during the service period. In addition, ERA paid for the training course fees (up to a ceiling) of participants who were working at least 16 hours per week.
- ERA advisers also had access to a small Emergency Discretion Fund to help participants with minor financial emergencies (e.g. special clothing) that could prevent them from retaining employment.

A cost-benefit analysis found that ERA was cost beneficial for long-term unemployed adult men, but not for lone parents. One possibility is that lone parents preferred to work part-time due to their childcare responsibilities. While the retention and advancement bonuses appear to have increased the hours of some participating lone parent, the effect tended to fade away once the bonuses were no longer available. This is not surprising, given the high marginal effective tax rates lone parents with additional expenditure on childcare face in the United Kingdom (see Box 3.9). Hence, lone parents would need either longer bonus periods or more extensive childcare subsidies.

Box 3.3. **Promoting employment retention and advancement in the United Kingdom** *(cont.)*

In-work support in the UK Work Programme

The UK *Work Programme* mainly refers long-term unemployed people to contracted providers, while short-term unemployed are still served by its PES. Different payment groups exist in the Work Programme, which are meant to reflect a jobseeker's relative level of difficulty in finding employment. The Work Programme payment model differs in a number of ways from Australia's model and places a higher focus on outcome fees. Two different types of outcome fees are available: job outcome payments and sustainment fees. Job outcome payments are made after participants spend three or six months of either continuous or cumulative spells in employment. Sustainment fees can be claimed every four weeks after the job-outcome payment for another 1-2 years. Sustainment fees account for 57% to 76% of providers' potential income for participants who started the Work Programme in 2011-12, with increasing relevance due to the elimination of upfront service fee and the reduced job outcome payments in subsequent years. The payment model therefore encourages providers to ensure job retention, which is associated with a number of longer-term benefits, including increased employment stability, skill acquisition, earnings growth, and career advancement.

An impact evaluation of the Work Programme is not available, but participant and provider surveys provide some useful insights for the design of payment models with longer term outcome payments. The participant survey showed that on average, half of the participants in work while on the Work Programme received in-work support. The support rates were higher for participants with caring responsibilities and those with long unemployment spells prior to employment. In-work support included advice from a personal adviser, help and support with benefits and financial advice, and contact with the employer to support the participant. However, providers did not use the sustainment payments to pay ERA-type retention bonuses. Also providers emphasised a need of in-work support for those who had been out of work for longer periods. In contrast, 30-39% of participants entering work avoided or refused the in-work support, possibly because they felt stigmatised by being on the Work Programme or wanted to feel that they had moved on from unemployment. The provider research also highlighted the administrative burden of providing evidence for sustainment payments and issues with the validation process, which will be important to address in the future.

Source: Bertram, C. et al. (2014), "Work Programme Evaluation: Operation of the commissioning model, finance and programme delivery", *Department for Work and Pensions Research Report*, No. 893, London; Greenberg, D., J. Walter and G. Knight (2013), "A Cost-benefit Analysis of the Random Assignment UK Employment Retention and Advancement Demonstration", *Applied Economics*, Vol. 45, No. 31, http://dx.doi.org/10.1080/00036846.2013.776664; Meager, N. et al. (2014), "Work Programme Evaluation: The Participant Experience Report", *Department for Work and Pensions Research Report*, No. 892, London; and OECD (2014), *Connecting People with Jobs: United Kingdom*, OECD Publishing, Paris, http://dx.doi.org/10.1787/9789264217188-en.

Facilitating job-to-job transitions of retrenched workers

Employment and activation policy in OECD countries tends to be concentrated on hard-to-place workers; in many cases increasingly so because of policy shifts aimed at bringing people with chronic health problems back into the labour market. This is true in many countries, including Australia, where employment services are perceived to be in place and prioritised for jobseekers most in need. This is a promising development insofar as some of those people have hitherto received little support and been parked on long-term or permanent benefits. However, this trend does have repercussions for workers who are more readily available for the labour market or available with less intense support.

One such group, typically, is retrenched workers: workers who have lost their job for economic reasons related to the business cycle, economic restructuring or globalisation, trade and offshoring. Many of these workers have had stable employment careers in the past and are maybe confronted with unemployment for the first time. The challenge for the labour market is to absorb these workers and the challenge for retrenched workers is to match their skills with the skills required in today's labour market. Australia has a flexible labour market that facilitates finding a new job in such situations although many people will only find casual employment or part-time employment and for those who have to accept wage cuts these can be substantial (OECD, 2016b). However, public policy to help those who do not find a new job themselves is less developed than in other OECD countries.

There are three main issues with the Australian approach vis-à-vis job retrenchment: i) special ad hoc assistance is concentrated on mass dismissals in certain sectors and regions whereas individual retrenchments or retrenchments from small businesses are left to the general system; ii) the general system is geared towards jobseekers entitled to means-tested benefits while other retrenched workers would receive limited employment support in their first year of unemployment; and iii) *jobactive* employment service providers generally lack expertise and incentives to support retrenched workers. Overall this implies that many retrenched workers in Australia receive little support, if any, and often very late. This is further accentuated for workers who receive severance pay which in the Australian context delays any possible entitlement to income support and, thus, implicitly employment support.

Australia could address some of those issues by looking at policies in other OECD countries although some of the problems in Australia are specific to the country context and the special setup of its system of benefits and employment services. More particularly, Australia could borrow ideas from a number of countries on how to reach workers retrenched individually or from smaller firms better and earlier (Box 3.4).

Box 3.4. **Policies aimed at reaching out to all retrenched workers early on**

Career Path Security Contracts in France: Since 2011, all permanent workers dismissed for economic reasons from a firm with less than 1 000 employees are entitled to a programme called *Contrat de sécurisation professionnelle* (CSP). The programme lasts up to 12 months and includes a range of measures aimed at improving re-employment prospects such as job-search assistance, intensive counselling, meeting a caseworker, skills evaluation, access to training, and follow-up support. The cost of the programme is shared between the public employment service, the employer and the employee, providing incentives for all actors to facilitate co-operation. The employer must offer the CSP to all workers they plan to dismiss before actual dismissal takes place and is subject to a significant fine in case of non-compliance. The workers participate in the cost by allocating part of their severance pay to the public employment service, waiving their notice period as well as their training rights acquired on the previous job (which are used to finance the CSP instead). Workers with at least one year of job tenure are provided higher benefits than other unemployed and can receive wage insurance if the new job pays less than 85% of the old job. Public employment service caseworkers are specialised experts who work exclusively with retrenched workers.

CRECs in Quebec: Quebec is the only province in Canada providing specialised adjustment assistance to workers affected by individual and small-scale dismissal. These workers can enrol in *Continuous-Entry Reclassification Committees* (CREC) which are open to all displaced workers from different firms and provide services similar to those otherwise provided in mass dismissals. CRECs meet the needs of regions: i) facing multiple redundancies in smaller firms with less than 50 displaced workers (the threshold necessary to qualify as large-scale dismissal), and/or ii) with limited public employment service capacity to cope with the sudden and massive influx of displaced workers in a local employment centre. To ensure sufficient capacity is available, the public employment service outsources these CREC outplacement services to specialised external providers. A permanent scheme such as CREC is advantageous due to its ability to i) rapidly meet the needs of displaced workers (which is more difficult for the regular employment service which, for example, may not have any vacancies for skilled workers); ii) deliver peer support because of shared experience between staff and clients; and iii) deliver services for bankrupt firms or runaway firms.

Box 3.4. **Policies aimed at reaching out to all retrenched workers early on** *(cont.)*

Job Security Councils in Sweden: *Job Security Councils* (JSC) were developed in the 1970s against the backdrop of the deteriorating economic conditions in Sweden and massive job losses of white-collar workers in the wake of the oil crisis in 1973. At that time, the Swedish public employment service was not regarded by employers as providing sufficient support for white-collar workers to find new jobs. JSCs, based on collective agreements between social partners in a sector or occupational field, are actively involved in the process of restructuring and provide advice and consultation to employers and trade unions at an early stage, while also providing transition services (individual counselling, career planning and job-search assistance) to redundant workers. JSC activities are financed by employer contributions (typically 0.3% of the payroll). JSCs distribute the risk and costs of restructuring among its members while allowing access for workers in small and medium enterprises. Around 80% of JSC participants find a solution (either employment or retraining) within a period of seven months, and this high number was sustained even during the crisis of 2008-10.

Warning pools in Denmark: Regardless of the size of a firm, warning pool funds can be used to establish a temporary employment service in a workplace, where caseworkers from the local Jobcentre deliver job-search assistance and help workers build a job strategy. Counselling services are provided *during* the notice period, preparing workers for their displacement. When the planned dismissals are of particular importance to the local community, additional funds are available. Supplementary warning pool funding can be granted to support retrenched workers *after* their notice period through counselling and clarification courses (up to two weeks), work-study programmes (internships and education) or language courses (up to eight months). Support for skills-upgrading is granted either for skills in current or future demand (as determined by the regional labour market authority). Skills-upgrading must be planned within 14 days after displacement, begin no later than three months after displacement and end at least six months after displacement.

Source: OECD (2015), *Back to Work: Canada: Improving the Re-employment Prospects of Displaced Workers*, Back to Work, OECD Publishing, Paris, http://dx.doi.org/10.1787/9789264233454-en; OECD (2015), *Back to Work: Sweden: Improving the Re-employment Prospects of Displaced Workers*, Back to Work, OECD Publishing, Paris, http://dx.doi.org/10.1787/23063831; and OECD (2016), *Back to Work: Denmark: Improving the Re-employment Prospects of Displaced Workers*, Back to Work, OECD Publishing, Paris, http://dx.doi.org/10.1787/23063831.

Aligning mutual obligations for mature age with those for younger jobseekers

As recognised in the *Intergenerational Report*, securing high levels of prosperity through economic growth will require increasing the labour market participation of mature age workers through encouraging them to stay in or re-enter work (Commonwealth of Australia, 2015). As set out by the OECD Council Recommendation on *Aging and Employment Policies* (OECD, 2016d), this requires i) strengthening financial incentives to carry on working; ii) tackling employment barriers on the side of employers; and iii) improving the employability of workers. Employment rates of mature age workers significantly increased over the past 15 years, indicating that Australia already made significant process in all of those areas (OECD, *forthcoming*). But there are still areas where Australia could strengthen its employment policies to boost labour market prospects for mature age workers. In order to improve the employability of workers throughout their working lives, Australia could take further steps to providing effective employment assistance to jobseekers, irrespective of their age, to ensure that mature age jobseekers have the same obligations as younger jobseekers for receiving unemployment benefits.

The initial set-up of Australia's jobactive employment services can be considered age-neutral. Allocation to different service streams, which in turn drive service intensity, is based on the jobseekers risk of remaining on income support for 12 months or more (see Box 3.2).[1] Providers are expected to tailor employment services to individual needs and circumstances to ensure that jobseekers are best placed to fill available jobs and meet their mutual obligation requirements. Mutual obligations for jobseekers in Australia, however, still vary by age: younger jobseekers under age 30 face stronger participation requirements than those over age 50.[2] Generally jobseekers are required to actively seek (and take up) paid work, which they must demonstrate through 20 job-search actions per month, unless their provider specifies a different number due to individual circumstances and labour market conditions. Furthermore, jobseekers have an activity requirement for six months each year while they remain unemployed. *Work for the Dole* is one of a number of approved activities that jobseekers may undertake to meet their mutual obligation requirement (see Box 3.2), which also include part-time work, voluntary work, or participation in accredited training courses. Mature age jobseekers have less stringent participation requirements (Department of Employment, 2014a):

- Jobseekers aged 50-59 years can choose which approved activity they will undertake as part of their annual activity requirement.
- Jobseekers aged 55-59 years are able to fully satisfy their participation requirements through undertaking 15 hours of voluntary work or paid work (or a combination of both) per week; they do not need to actively seek employment whilst engaged in voluntary or paid work.
- Jobseekers aged 60 years and over have job-search requirements tailored to their individual circumstances and have no annual activity requirement, but can choose to volunteer.

Around 13% of mature age jobseekers fully meet their participation requirements through voluntary or paid work. Abolishing the exemptions for older unemployed has been previously recommended (e.g. OECD, 2012a) and the Department of Employment aimed to make necessary changes to the Social Security Act 1991 (Department of Employment, 2014b). At the time of writing these exceptions are, however, still in place and they should be reconsidered once again in light of experiences in providing effective employment assistance to mature age jobseekers in other countries.

The Netherlands abolished special rules exempting older unemployed people from active job search in 2004. Research found that prior to the abolition of these special rules, older unemployed already reduced their job-search efforts when getting close to the threshold age in anticipation of the imminent relief from their job-search obligations. The abolition of this exemption in job-search obligations resulted in increased off-flows into employment, but also in an increase in the number of individuals transitioning to disability benefits (Box 3.5). Given the less stringent participation requirements, lower job-finding rates for older unemployed are likely to prevail in Australia. OECD (2012a) reports that service providers regard the suspension of job-search requirements while doing voluntary work as a lost opportunity for service delivery. The Dutch case shows accompanying measures are required to achieve the expected outcomes. One such measure already in place in Australia is the *Restart* employment subsidy, an incentive payment of up to AUD 10 000 available to employers who hire a jobseeker aged 50 years or older who has been unemployed and on income support for a minimum of six months (Department of Employment, 2014a).

A recent pilot programme in Switzerland shows that providing extra support to mature age workers may help to address their relatively weaker labour market position.

The programme provided intensive counselling and a coaching seminar and had a clear positive impact on re-employment rates of jobseekers aged 45-54 years. However, the programme did not have an impact on those over age 55 (Box 3.5). Given Australia's geographical size, including some very remote labour markets, and against the background of older retrenched workers particularly struggling with labour market reintegrating, the Canadian *Targeted Initiative for Older Workers (TIOW)* may be of particular interest. The programme is designed to support unemployed mature age workers living in small, vulnerable communities of less than 250 000 inhabitants. Although not targeted at Indigenous Canadians, some TIOW projects have a high proportion of Indigenous Canadians among their participants, which in turn may also drive the programme curriculum (again, Box 3.5).

Box 3.5. **Providing employment assistance to mature age jobseekers in the Netherlands, Switzerland and Canada**

Increasing mutual obligations for mature age workers in the Netherlands

In the Netherlands, the maximum duration for unemployment insurance benefits has been shortened considerably, from previously five years to 38 months in 2006. Since the beginning of 2016 the maximum duration is further reduced by one month each quarter to eventually reach 24 months in April 2019. The aim of these subsequent reforms was to increase the job-search incentives, and shorten the periods of inactivity, which is a particular concern for mature age workers. While having reduced the maximum benefit duration, the Netherlands also abolished special rules exempting unemployed people over the age of 57.5 from reporting job-search efforts to the Public Employment Service (PES) at the beginning of 2004. From then on, all new benefit recipients aged 57.5 to 64 years are – just like younger recipients – required to actively search for a job and undertake a minimum of four job-search activities per month which must be reported to the PES in regular intervals. Those over 64 are still exempt from job search (Langenbucher, 2014).

Hullegie and van Ours (2013) found that the exemption from job-search requirements for older recipients prior to 2004 resulted in a clear negative anticipation effect, in the sense that the job finding rate of unemployed workers who were getting close to the age of 57.5 was reduced in anticipation of the removal of the search requirement. The actual exception resulted in a further large negative effect. Using data only up to one year after the policy change, they find a relatively small increase in the job-finding rates after the introduction of the job-search requirements, a fact that they relate to the relatively weak labour market position of mature age workers. Using data for a longer period (up to 2008), Koning and Raterink (2013) found that both the policy reform in 2004 and the reduction of the maximum duration of unemployment benefits in 2006 have increased job return rates for those unemployed above the age of 55, with the impact of the job-search requirement being larger. Lammers et al. (2013) in turn studied how the changes in search requirements affected the transition rates to employment and to sickness and disability benefits. Their main finding is that the reform contributed to a 6-(11)-percentage point increase in the number of male (female) individuals who found a job. However, this strong, positive effect on labour market participation is accompanied by a 4-(9)-percentage point increase in the number of male (female) individuals receiving disability benefits within 24 months after the start of the unemployment spell. Hence, the substitution effects of this Dutch reform were substantial.

The project "preventing long-term unemployment" in Switzerland

In 2007/08 the Swiss canton of Aargau ran a randomised control trial for unemployed aged 45 to 63 years, providing them with intensive counselling and a coaching seminar to support them in more effective job-search. The intensive counselling provided programme participants with fortnightly intensive counselling session for the first four months of unemployment, instead of the usual monthly sessions. The coaching seminar lasted a total of 20 days spread over around eight weeks. For groups of 10-15 participants the seminar covered targeted training on labour market competences, improving job search, assessing a potential re-orientation of the job search towards different positions, self-motivation and marketing oneself, and it gave participants a heavy load of homework. The intention was for participants to access the seminar after 50 days of unemployment, but programme start dates varied between 0 and 290 days of unemployment.

Box 3.5. Providing employment assistance to mature age jobseekers in the Netherlands, Switzerland and Canada *(cont.)*

Overall, the evaluation of Arni (2012) finds a positive impact of the project. For participants aged 45-54 years, there is a clear positive effect of the intensive counselling and the coaching seminar on the re-employment rate, but not so for those aged over 55. The programme did not impact the duration of unemployment, which Arni assess as a positive result, as it shows that the lock-in effect – usually associated with training programme – is weak. The impact on the rate of long-term unemployment, however, was weak even though programme participants were more likely to find work. On the more positive side, the evaluation results show that the stability of post-unemployment jobs increased, resulting in a reduction of future unemployment spells by 20 days on average. In fact, the realised savings in unemployment insurance expenditure outweighed the costs of the programme. The study also shows that the jobseekers reduced the intensity of their job search in anticipation of participation in the coaching seminar, which also resulted in lower flows off benefit. However, this negative impact on the re-employment rate was lower or could be avoided altogether for those allocated to the seminar earlier on in their unemployment spell. Another important effect of the programme was that the coaching seminar helped jobseekers to develop more realistic expectations for future employment, especially with respect of income they would be willing to accept. At first, both jobseekers and counsellors tend to overestimate the chances of reintegration. More realistic expectations have a positive effect on job search, especially as the participants were more motivated due to the intensive counselling and the coaching seminar.

The Targeted Initiative for Older Workers in Canada

Canada's Targeted Initiative for Older Workers (TIOW) programme is a federal-provincial/territorial cost-shared initiative specifically designed to support unemployed mature age workers in re-integrating into employment and/or becoming more employable. TIOW targets unemployed aged 55 to 64, living in small, vulnerable communities of 250 000 inhabitants or less, and affected by high unemployment or significant downsizing or firm closures. The last renewal of the programme for the period 2014-17 broadened the eligibility criteria to also support communities experiencing unfulfilled employer demand and/or skills mismatches. Since 2007, TIOW has provided support to over 35 000 unemployed mature age workers in over 800 projects (as of March 2015) and the average cost per programme participant is estimated at about CAD 7 000. Under TIOW agreements, the Government of Canada contributes up to 70% of programme costs and each province and/or territory contributes a minimum of 30%. The majority of TIOW projects are delivered by third-party community-based organisations, but the precise delivery model varies across provinces and territories.

TIOW projects provide group-based skills training and employment assistance services. TIOW participants are also offered income support in the form of allowances during the training. TIOW projects offer at least 25 hours of training per week, and must include employment assistance services (such as job-search techniques, CV writing, interview techniques and counselling) and at least two employability improvement activities (such as basic skills upgrading, vocational skill training, work-experience, direct marketing to employers and preparation for self-employment). The latest evaluation of TIOW indicates that 75% of all participants found paid employment following their participation in TIOW. In comparison with a group of unemployed receiving the mainstream employment assistance services, the net impact of the programme on employment is positive (TIOW increases re-employment rates by six percentages points) but it has no impact on earnings and the use of Employment Insurance or Social Assistance. The programme also succeeds in reaching vulnerable mature age workers: half of TIOW participants had not attained more than a high school diploma (including 24% not having completed high school) and half of the participants experienced a recent job loss, either in the year they started the TIOW programme or in the year before. Given the large number of individual TIOW projects, the programme also ensures that best practices between the different projects are shared through yearly best practices workshops and a best practices compendium containing three broad themes: i) innovative project design and administration, ii) working with employers, and iii) building on local strengths.

Box 3.5. **Providing employment assistance to mature age jobseekers in the Netherlands, Switzerland and Canada** *(cont.)*

The Fort St. James TIOW project

Fort St. James is a small community in north central British Columbia, 160 kilometres northwest of Prince George, the nearest major city. It is the service hub for a broader district of around 3 000 people with about half living in the town itself and half living on reserves in four First Nations communities. The Fort St. James population is younger, has less educational attainment and is also somewhat more reliant on public income support than the provincial average. Forestry, mining and exploration are the main economic drivers. Employment in these sectors can vary to a large extend depending on world commodity prices.

As part of the 2014-17 programme period the Government of British Columbia selected the Fort St. James project as one of 14 TIOW projects in the province. Fort St. James had managed seven earlier intakes of TIOW projects from 2009 to 2012, with about a dozen participants per wave. 77 of the 83 participants were of First People ancestry. A common factor among all participants was reportedly a lack of self-confidence about their overall workplace literacy skills and, for many, a lack of high school diploma. The profile of programme participants in earlier TIOW waves included many experienced workers who were laid off as a result of mill closures associated with the economic downturn of 2008. While earlier waves had an emphasis on literacy skills and employability, participants in subsequent waves tended to face more health and social barriers to work and, as a result, First Nations Wellness workers have been included in the programme curriculum. Despite the poor economic situation following the economic downturn, the project reported positive outcomes for most participants. Participants became more employable and 53% of those who completed the programme subsequently found jobs, although this included part-time and seasonal work.

Source: Arni, P. (2011): "Langzeitarbeitslosigkeit verhindern: Intensivberatung und -coaching für ältere Stellensuchende – ein Weg zu verbesserten Arbeitsmarktchancen?" [Preventing long-term unemployment: Intensive counseling and coaching for mature age jobseekers – a path towards improved labour market opportunities?], Office for Economy and Labour [Amt für Wirtschaft und Arbeit] of the Canton of Aargau and University of Lausanne; Employment and Social Development Canada (2014), "Summative Evaluation of the Targeted Initiative for Older Workers", Final Report, Partnership Evaluation, Evaluation Directorate Strategic Policy and Research Branch, 5 May; Goldman, L. (2015), "The Canadian Targeted Initiative for Older Workers (TIOW)", OECD LEED Expert Roundtable: Local economic strategies for ageing labour markets, 31 March, http://www.oecd.org/cfe/leed/roundtable-ageing-labour-markets.htm; Hicks, P. (2015), "Local Economic Strategies for Ageing Labour Markets: The Canadian Targeted Initiative for Older Workers in Fort St. James, British Columbia", *OECD Local Economic and Employment Development (LEED) Working Papers*, 2015/03, OECD Publishing, Paris, http://dx.doi.org/10.1787/5jrnwqk5d4f7-en; Hullegie, P. and J.C. van Ours (2013), "Seek and Ye Shall Find: How Search Requirements Affect Job Finding Rates of Older Workers", *IZA Discussion Paper*, No. 7400, IZA, Bonn; Koning, P. and M. Raterink (2013), "Re-employment Rates of Older Unemployed Workers: Decomposing the Effect of Birth Cohorts and Policy Changes", *De Economist*, Vol. 161, http://dx.doi.org/10.1007/s10645-013-9208-2; Lammers, M., H. Bloemen and S. Hochguertel (2013), "Job Search Requirements for Older Unemployed: Transitions to Employment, Early Retirement and Disability Benefits", *European Economic Review*, Vol. 58; Langenbucher, K. (2015), "How Demanding Are Eligibility Criteria for Unemployment Benefits. Quantitative Indicators for OECD and EU Countries", *OECD Social, Employment and Migration Working Papers*, No. 166, OECD Publishing, Paris, http://dx.doi.org/10.1787/5jrxtk1zw8f2-en; OECD (2015), *Back to Work: Canada: Improving the Re-employment Prospects of Displaced Workers*, OECD Publishing, Paris, http://dx.doi.org/10.1787/9789264233454-en; and OECD (2014), *Ageing and Employment Policies: Netherlands 2014: Working Better with Age*, OECD Publishing. http://dx.doi.org/10.1787/9789264208155-en.

Policies to better harness the work capacity of people with a disability

Across OECD countries too many workers leave the labour market permanently because of chronic ill-health or disability and too few people with reduced work capacity manage to find a job. Australia is no exception: Nearly 6% of the working-age population receive a de facto permanent disability benefit (see Figure 1.15) and only 40% of all people with a disability are employed, compared to 78% of people without a disability (see Figure 1.14). At 38 percentage points, the disability gap in employment is the second largest in the OECD area (after the United States and more than 10 percentage points larger than the OECD average gap), and it has increased in the past 15 years. Notably, anti-discrimination legislation which is probably more developed in Australia and the United States than in any other OECD country has not helped to reduce the employment gap.

The situation could be addressed in two ways: by i) helping people with disability into the labour market and ii) helping employed people with chronic health problems or disability retain their jobs. While both types of policies are needed, international evidence suggests that job retention policies are both cheaper and much more effective than job creation policies (OECD, 2010). For a long time, disability policy across the OECD area and also in Australia has overlooked the potential of retention policies. Disability policy was perceived as social policy with very limited employment focus, and disability benefit therefore a payment from which there was no return to the labour market, even if it was initially granted temporarily. In the past 15 years, further pushed by early work of the OECD (OECD, 2003), the focus of disability policy has gradually changed, and broadened. Also in Australia, disability benefit reform in the recent past was characterised by a shift towards a stronger labour market focus with increased participation requirements for people with partial work capacity who are now obliged to look for (part-time) employment in line with their partial capacity.

Other than this, evidence from other OECD countries shows that two things matter especially for retention policies to be effective: i) early intervention – the earlier the better – because the likelihood to stay in work or return to work falls very quickly when workers are away from the labour market for health reasons or disability for too long; and ii) obligations and incentives for all actors – workers, employers, doctors, service providers, public authorities – aligned towards the same objective: to increase employment opportunities for individuals with a disability. There is room for Australia to improve its policies on both accounts, especially in regard to sickness absence policy and management which is not considered a public affair and left predominantly to the judgement of doctors and voluntary actions of employers.

Earlier intervention can be promoted in many different ways common to which is the goal to help people who need help quickly to prevent long-term sickness absence, early labour market exit and disability benefit claims. Some countries do this by recognising and closing the gap between employer action to help people return from a sick leave and support available when people apply for a disability benefit. Both Austria and the United Kingdom have put in place a new structure of services aimed at making people who struggle with health issues fit for work again as quickly as possible by providing or organising the necessary return-to-work case management support (Box 3.6). Lacking any public intervention in this phase, Australia could consider putting in place a similar structure.

Other OECD countries have used other approaches to tackle the often steep increase in disability benefit caseloads in recent decades. Countries are moving away from merely compensating work disability towards activating claimants to help them return to the world of work. In Switzerland this was done by involving the disability insurance in the process at an earlier stage so as to activate people at risk of dropping out from the labour market before it is too late (Box 3.7). The Danish Government went one step further, concluding that more needs to be done especially for young adults with chronic health problems or disability with little or no work experience who should not claim and be granted a disability benefit until all efforts to help them into a (regular or subsidised) job have failed. The new approach in Denmark can be described as early vocational rehabilitation building on the individual's resources, with integrated health and employment support (again, Box 3.7). Through these reforms, both Switzerland and Denmark, contrary to Australia, invest considerable public funds into helping people with chronic health problems or disability find, stay in, or return to employment in recognition of the disadvantage this group is facing in today's fast-changing, high-performing labour market.

Box 3.6. **Public sickness policy in Austria and the United Kingdom aimed at supporting the return to work of longer-term sick workers quickly and effectively**

Austria's fit2work service

Few firms in Austria take any measures to follow up on employees on long-term sick leave. Sickness absence in Austria follows an all-or-nothing principle: the lack of a gradual return-to-work process is a barrier to resuming employment. In order to provide greater return-to-work support for people on long-term sick leave, the Austrian Government – together with the social partners and the social insurance providers – has initiated a new low-threshold information, counselling and support service for sick-listed employees and jobseekers as well as enterprises. The new fit2work service, fully implemented in 2013, seeks to avert job losses and long-term unemployment. Health insurance contacts sick-listed employees after around 40 days of absence, offering general information (on possible treatment, for example), counselling and return-to-work support by a network of counselling firms. Waiting times for health services (e.g. psychotherapy) can also be reduced.

Initial evaluations show that only around one-quarter of all sick-listed people who were contacted and given information, considered to be counselled by a fit2work provider and a much lower share of only around 10% actually contacted a provider. Fit2work's rationale of increasing sick workers' job retention and reintegrating unemployed people with health problems is valuable in view of Austria's weak focus on sickness absence. To strengthen the impact of the service, the link with the health system needs to be strengthened; direct workplace-focused counselling be expanded; and reaching out to employers be prioritised.

The United Kingdom's Fit for Work Service

The Fit for Work Service (FFWS) was piloted in several regions in the United Kingdom from April 2010 to March 2013. Its chief aim was to provide personalised back-to-work support for people in the early stages of sickness absence (4-12 weeks of absence) and reduce the drift into welfare benefits. The pilots brought together health, employment and local community organisations and offered biopsychosocial assessments of need and case-managed support to aid quick return to work. The service targeted people in work with a health condition, including those on sick leave and those at risk of sickness absence. Case managers offered support with goal setting, progress monitoring, confidence-building, motivation, and other forms of assistance. Individuals could access FFWS by being referred by their general practitioner or other health service providers, or through self-referral.

Over the first year, take-up was significantly lower than expected. In most pilots, mental health conditions were the most commonly reported condition and many clients had more than one health condition. The average length of time people stayed with the service was four months. The full FFWS, implemented in 2014, builds upon the pilot schemes. The new service will provide a work-focused biopsychosocial assessment to employees earlier in their sickness absence spell – from around four weeks of absence onwards. It also offers advice to employers and employees on needs for rehabilitation and return-to-work support for both workers on sick leave and those still at work.

Source: Egger-Subotitsch, A. and M. Stark (2013), *Fit2work Implementierungsevaluierung* [Evaluation of the implementation of fit2work], Bundessozialamt, Vienna; OECD (2015), *Mental Health and Work: Austria*, OECD Publishing, Paris, http://dx.doi.org/10.1787/9789264228047-en; Hillage, J. et al. (2012), "Evaluation of the Fit for Work Service Pilots: First Year Report", *DWP Research Report*, No. 792, London; and OECD (2013), *Mental Health and Work: United Kingdom*, OECD Publishing, Paris, http://dx.doi.org/10.1787/9789264204997-en.

Box 3.7. Early intervention, activation and rehabilitation in Switzerland and Denmark to prevent disability benefit claims

Early intervention by the Swiss disability insurance

A sharp increase in disability benefit claims since the 1990s led to a series of revisions of the Swiss Invalidity Insurance Act. The 5th revision, in 2008, switched the strong focus on invalidity benefit to the ability to work. The reform reinforced the emphasis on vocational rehabilitation, added a new focus on job retention, and implemented a paradigm shift in the invalidity insurance's focus to early identification and activation of potential claimants. The main measures introduced by the reform were: i) early notification of problems to the invalidity insurance, by the employer, the employee, the treating doctor, or any other stakeholder; ii) new early intervention measures to secure job retention or help claimants find a new job (workplace adaptations, educational courses, active job placement, vocational counselling, social-vocational rehabilitation, and activation; all measures require an assessment and a binding rehabilitation plan); and iii) substantial wage subsidies for employers hiring a disability benefit claimant (subsidies may be paid for half a year at up to 100% of the salary if the claimant has not regained full work capacity).

An early evaluation of the effects of the new early intervention measures showed that through the reform, the share of claimants back in employment 18 months after their initial contact with the cantonal invalidity authority increased from 40% to 44%. Claimants still employed when they first contacted the invalidity authority had a much higher reemployment rate than unemployed claimants (55% versus 30% were employed 18 months later), confirming the need for early intervention.

The Danish resource process for people under age 40

In response to the large and growing number of young adults under the age of 25 moving to claim a disability benefit, the Danish Government has made a major reform to the disability scheme. The intention is to largely abolish disability benefit for the under-40s (unless they are totally unable to work), replacing it with a new rehabilitation model, also called resource process, whose chief features are that: i) the health sector, labour market institutions, social services and the education sector are involved, with responsibility lying with the municipal job centre; ii) an interdisciplinary rehabilitation team is established in every municipality to ensure the integrated approach will work in practice; iii) the rehabilitation team discusses needs, makes recommendations, and co-ordinates actions, although decisions are taken jointly by every institution towards an agreed goal; iv) it lasts for up to five years depending on the client's needs; v) it involves a co-ordinator, whose role is to co-ordinate action and steer clients through the system; and vi) during rehabilitation, people continue to receive whatever benefit they are on or, if not entitled to any, a minimum income at the social assistance level.

The new model aims to ensure treatment where necessary, with work seen as part of the solution. It is focused neither on assessing the degree of illness (the health sector view) nor the work capability (the job centre view), but on integrating those approaches. The success of the reform will depend on the way it is implemented. Initial results suggest there is a chance that the reform may achieve at least some of its aims: it has more than halved the number of new disability benefit claims. Most of those people no longer entitled to disability benefit are engaged in the new resource process. However, until today only a small minority of those people have found a job and of those who did, most are in subsidised employment. It is too early to tell whether a sufficiently large number of people will eventually be reintegrated into the labour market in a sustainable manner.

Source: Bolliger, C. et al. (2012), "Eingliederung vor Rente. Evaluation der Früherfassung und der Integrationsmassnahmen in der Invalidenversicherung" [Rehabilitation Before Pension. Evaluation of Early Detection and Integration Measures in the Disability Insurance], FoP-IV Forschungsbericht, Bundesamt für Sozialversicherungen, Bern; OECD (2014), *Mental Health and Work: Switzerland*, OECD Publishing, Paris, http://dx.doi.org/10.1787/9789264204973-en; OECD (2013), *Mental Health and Work: Denmark*, OECD Publishing, Paris, http://dx.doi.org/10.1787/9789264188631-en; TheDanishGovernment (2013), "The National Reform Programme Denmark 2013", Copenhagen; and The Danish Government (2012), "The National Reform Programme Denmark 2012", Copenhagen.

Another critical issue is the role of general practitioners and in particular their implicit role as gatekeepers for the benefit system and therefore as facilitators for labour market exit more generally. Doctors tend to grant sick-leave certificates easily and with a view on a patient's health, without any consideration of work factors and labour market implications, despite plenty of evidence pointing towards the value of good work for people's health and recovery. Several OECD countries, including Australia, have changed the way they assess people's work capacity and ability (rather than disability) in the process of a disability benefit claim, implying tighter access for people with partial capacity. Some countries have also reduced the role of treating doctors in order to objectify the process. Countries have struggled more with influencing the quality of sickness certificates which are still in the hands of an individual's treating doctor. Sweden has introduced illness-specific guidelines for the certification process which are binding for treating doctors, and the United Kingdom has replaced the previous sick note with a new fit note to increase the treating doctor's attention to work-related matters (Box 3.8). Both approaches could also be adopted in the Australian context.

Policies to stimulate labour demand for people with a disability have seen less success in the current labour market context, and typically such policies are also very costly (OECD, 2010). Some OECD countries, especially the Nordic countries, have invested greatly in flexible, subsidised employment. These policies have seen some success but countries have also struggled to reach the right group of people through these subsidies. Subsidies need to be targeted tightly because they can lead to subsidising part-time work of people able to work full time, rather than encouraging people with low work capacity to access the labour market (OECD, 2013b). Other countries have invested considerably in sheltered employment and the creation of a second labour market. This is generally helping only a small number of people and for a very high cost per capita. Yet other countries – especially in central and southern Europe as well as Asia – use mandatory disability employment quotas, typically in the range of 2-6% of the workforce, requiring firms to employ a certain number of people with a disability or otherwise pay a fine for circumventing this obligation (which empirically the majority of firms choose to do). Evidence suggests that most demand side-oriented policies, including anti-discrimination legislation mentioned earlier, tend to help people who have a job stay in their job more than they help outsiders to access the labour market (OECD, 2003; OECD, 2010).

It is probably not the moment for Australia to introduce any new demand-side policies in the disability field now, in the midst of the roll-out of the *National Disability Insurance Scheme* which will begin in January 2017 (https://www.ndis.gov.au/). The new scheme means an overhaul of the entire approach with considerable additional investment to empower people with a significant disability. It remains to be seen whether that investment will in the longer run also result in higher participation and employment rates for the group targeted by the scheme.

Box 3.8. **Measures in Sweden and the United Kingdom aimed at strengthening the work focus of general practitioners**

Work-focused sickness certification guidelines for doctors in Sweden

In 2005 the Swedish National Board of Health and Welfare developed new ways to improve the quality of sickness certification in an effort to reduce high levels of sickness absence. To date, the board has published 120 illness-specific guidelines which include criteria for judging individual cases – e.g. expected prognosis, effective treatment, and the length of sickness absence. The guidelines are based on a combination of scientific evidence and consensus among different specialists. For example, the guidelines on depression recommend that people with uncomplicated first-time depression can achieve improved functionality within three months of adequate treatment.

The newly developed diagnosis-specific medical guidelines have had a significant impact on the attitude towards prescribing sick leave. Evidence suggests that sickness absence guidelines for the most frequent illnesses have contributed to a much reduced incidence and shorter spells of sickness absence and a much narrower distribution of diagnoses. In a recent national survey of all general practitioners, around 76% reported the use of national sickness guidelines. Nearly two-thirds reported that the guidelines had facilitated their contacts with patients and one-third spoke of improved communication with social insurance officers, other health care staff, and employers.

Fit notes in the United Kingdom requiring increased work-related knowledge

Since 2010, general practitioners have had to provide a Statement of Fitness for Work (known as "fit note" in place of the previous "sick note") across England, Wales and Scotland. Doctors are now not only required to assess whether their patients are able to work but to suggest basic changes to the work environment or job role, or other steps to help employees return to work earlier. For instance, if a patient is classified in the "maybe fit for work" category, the doctor is required to specify at least one of four options outlining common return-to-work approaches – a phased return to work; amended duties; altered hours; and workplace adaptations. Doctors are also required to assess a patient's fitness for (any) work rather than fitness for a specific job. The changes also mean a move towards an electronic fit note which, in theory, should generate new, standardised data (including on causes of absence) and bring transparency to a hitherto rather undisclosed process.

Qualitative evaluations suggest that the fit note is being used by general practitioners to initiate discussions about work with their patients and that it has also improved the information flow between employers and employees. Although fit notes have facilitated dialogue between doctors, employees and employers, there is a long way to go to make the most from the new approach. One particular challenge for better use of the fit note is the lack of workplace knowledge among doctors. Challenges also remain in issuing fit notes for those with mental health conditions. There is some evidence that because they have little knowledge of mental health conditions and interact little with workplaces, doctors have a greater tendency to write patients with poor mental health off sick for longer periods.

Source: OECD (2013), *Mental Health and Work: Sweden*, OECD Publishing, Paris, http://dx.doi.org/10.1787/9789264188730-en; Skaner, Y. et al. (2011), "Use and Usefulness of Guidelines for Sickness Certification: Results from a National Survey of All General Practitioners in Sweden", *BMJ Open*, Vol. 1, No. 1; Chenery, V. (2013), "An Evaluation of the Statement of Fitness for Work: A Survey of Employees", *DWP Research Report*, No. 840, London; OECD (2013a), *Mental Health and Work: United Kingdom*, OECD Publishing, Paris, http://dx.doi.org/10.1787/9789264204997-en; and Shiels, C. et al. (2013), "An Evaluation of the Statement of Fitness for Work: Quantitative Survey of Fit Notes", *DWP Research Report*, No. 841, London.

Helping more lone parents to access employment

Australia used to provide means-tested income support to lone parents with very few conditions attached. The Welfare to Work reform in 2006 introduced participation requirements for principle carer parents – i.e. lone parents or the principle carer in couple families – once the youngest child turns six.[3] At this point, principle carer parents claiming income support have part-time mutual obligation requirements, which amount to about half of the hours required for other jobseekers on income support: they must be actively looking for suitable part-time work of at least 15 hours per week, or undertaking other approved activities.[4] When their youngest child turns eight, lone parents are transferred from Parenting Payment to Newstart Allowance which is around 30% lower.

Principal carer parents meeting their mutual obligation requirements through 30 hours per fortnight of paid work or approved study, and in some circumstances voluntary work or a combination of these activities, cannot be required to participate in Work for the Dole (or undertake any other activity or job search requirements). Others can choose to undertake Work for the Dole to meet their requirements, but a principal carer parent would not be required to attend any activity outside of their home during the school holidays where appropriate care and supervision of their children is not available.

Changes to benefit entitlement and participation requirements initially only affected new claimants, while those with an existing Parenting Payment entitlement were "grandfathered", i.e. potentially not affected by the reforms until their youngest child turned 16. From mid-2007, however, participation requirements were also phased in gradually for "grandfathered" claimants with a youngest child over age seven over a transition period of around twelve months.

Principle carer parents on income support with a youngest child under age six have very few obligations, apart from an annual interview with Centrelink. They can take-up support services from the contracted employment service providers as "volunteers", but the services they receive are limited in comparison to jobseekers with job-search requirements. Volunteers receive time-limited services of up to six months helping them understand and navigate the labour market and write a CV, or referring them to suitable vacancies. Provider fees for such volunteers are rather low, as they only attract fees of work-ready jobseekers (see Box 3.2) (Department of Employment, 2014a).

Evaluations of the Welfare to Work reforms in 2006 and 2007 found positive impacts for lone parents with older children with respect to flows off income support (Fok and McVicar, 2013) and into employment (Gong and Breunig, 2014), at least initially. Lone mother employment rates increased after the 2006 reform to reach a peak of 57% in 2008. Thereafter, however, these rates dropped again and in 2014 they were not higher than in 2006. In contrast, employment rates of partnered mothers continued to grow over the same period (see Figure 1.9, Panel B). The analysis in Chapter 2 shows that lone parents persistently out of the labour market face a range of employment barriers including low education or skills, long-standing physical or mental health conditions and a lack of work experience. This suggests that additional measures are needed to achieve a lasting increase in lone parent labour market participation.

The activation policy stance towards lone parents varies to a great deal across the OECD. For Australia, there are useful insights to gain both from countries with a similar stance and those with a markedly different approach. Australia, together with Ireland, the Netherlands, New Zealand and the United Kingdom, had lone mother employment rates of below 50% in the early 2000s (see Figure 1.9). All countries provide non-time-limited, means-tested income support, with net replacement rates for the long-term unemployed of 60% or more. An income support work-test (i.e. a requirement to be available for work or training) now exists in all five countries for lone parents with older children, but the participation requirements are mainly part-time[5] and only around half or less of lone mothers in these countries work full-time – with the exception of New Zealand. Out-of-pocket childcare costs tend to be high (Table 3.1). In 2014, employment rates of lone mothers in these countries are still low both in an international comparison and in comparison to partnered mothers in the respective countries.

This contrasts with countries that use an active stance towards all parents, including Austria, Denmark, Finland, France, Germany, Luxembourg, Slovenia, Sweden, and Switzerland, where lone mother employment rates are close to or above the OECD average (again, see Figure 1.9). In most of these countries the majority of lone mothers also work full-time, except for Austria and Germany (see Figure 1.6). Net replacement rates for long-term unemployed lone parents are among the highest in the OECD. These countries generally apply a full-time work test when the youngest child turns three or even before and childcare costs tend to be relatively low (Table 3.1).

Reforms in OECD countries which until recently also had a weak activation stance on lone parents, provide useful insights for Australia (Box 3.9). The introduction of a work test in New Zealand and the United Kingdom once their youngest child reaches compulsory school age resulted in a reduction of lone parents claiming income support and in increases in lone parent employment rates. Especially the UK reforms seem to have resulted in a lasting increase in lone parent employment following the labour market recovery after 2011 (see Figure 1.9, Panel B). Neither of the two countries "grandfathered" existing claims. In New Zealand, the positive results may also be driven by an increased focus of the public employment service on the lone parent client group. However, experience from the United Kingdom also highlights the risk of an increase in claims for health-related benefits and non-claimant unemployment. The reforms reported in Box 3.9 mainly resulted in an increase in part-time employment, which is different to the mainly full-time employment achieved in most countries with an active stance towards all parents. In New Zealand and the United Kingdom lone parents, however, have weak financial incentives to work longer hours, which often is the result of a lack of affordable, good quality childcare to cover longer working hours. A measure recently introduced in Ireland aims to enable low-income families to work beyond the usual school hours through providing low-cost after school hours childcare for up to one year.

Table 3.1. **Labour market outcomes for lone parents: The result of a different mixture of policies**

Country	Employment rates for mothers (aged 15-64) with at least one child aged 0-15: Partnered mothers, Employment rates (%), 2014 [a]	Lone mothers, Employment rates (%), 2014 [a]	Lone mothers, Part-time share (%), 2013 [b]	Benefit generosity if unemployed: Net Replacement Rates[c] for previous earnings at 67% of average wage, 2014	Income support work test: Age of youngest child when work test applies	Net childcare costs with two children [d]: Out-of-pocket costs for full-time care [e], 2012, % of family net income
Formerly low activation stance for lone parents						
Australia	65.5	50.8	48.6	62.0	From age 6	14.1
Ireland	63.3	46.2	53.2	65.6	From age 14	41.6
Netherlands	77.1	59.3	75.4	61.4	From age 5	12.9
New Zealand	65.8	53.7	37.2	64.2	From age 5	20.5
United Kingdom	70.1	58.5	56.2	72.6	From age 5	7.9
Generally active stance towards all parents						
Austria	76.4	71.3	59.5	84.1	From age 3	5.6
Denmark	84.6	74.3	21.2	84.4	Discretion, generally after parental leave (age 1)	2.9
Finland	74.0	65.3	17.0	74.2	Discretion, generally after home care leave (age 3)	17.1
France	74.1	63.1	27.5	63.3	From age 3 [f]	4.4
Germany	69.5	66.8	54.9	73.1	From age 3	5.2
Luxembourg	73.5	85.3	29.0	75.7	From age 6	3.2
Slovenia	80.1	70.0	9.4	70.3		16.1
Sweden	84.6	74.8	24.3	60.1	Discretion, generally after parental leave (16 mo.)	4.2
Switzerland	76.6	86.3		76.3	Varies across Cantons	10.6

a) Data for Denmark and Finland refer to 2012 and for Germany to 2013. For Sweden employment rates are for women aged 15-74 with children aged 0-18.

b) Data for Australia refer to 2011; for Denmark, Finland and Sweden to 2012.

c) Net replacement rates are in the 60th month of benefit receipt, after tax and including unemployment and family benefits for a lone parent with 2 children qualifying for cash housing assistance or social assistance "top ups" if available. Social assistance and other means-tested benefits are assumed to be available subject to relevant income conditions. Housing costs are assumed equal to 20% of AW. Where receipt of social assistance or other minimum-income benefits is subject to activity tests (such as active job-search or being "available" for work), these requirements are assumed to be met. Children are aged four and six and neither childcare benefits nor childcare costs are considered.

d) Children aged 2 and 3 years and the lone parents full-time earnings are at 67% of the average wage.

e) Data refer to the following regions: England for the United Kingdom, Vienna for Austria, Helsinki for Finland, Hamburg for Germany and Zurich for Switzerland.

f) For France the work test applies to the Social Assistance (RMI) supplement when parents are in activation programmes; until the youngest child is aged 3 lone parents can claim Sole parent benefit (API), where there is no work test.

Source: **Maternal employment rates**: *OECD Family Database*, The labour market position of families, LMF1.3 Maternal employment by partnership status, http://www.oecd.org/social/family/database.htm. **Lone mothers, incidence of part-time employment**: *OECD Family Database*, The labour market position of families, LMF2.3 Maternal employment by partnership status, http://www.oecd.org/social/family/database.htm. **Benefit generosity and net childcare costs**: OECD, Tax-Benefit Models. **Income support work test**: OECD (2014a) for United Kingdom; Department of Social Protection of Ireland (2016a) for Ireland; OECD (2014d) for New Zealand; OECD (2011) for all other countries.

StatLink http://dx.doi.org/10.1787/888933447560

Box 3.9. Recent reforms to lone parent employment policies in New Zealand, the United Kingdom and Ireland

New Zealand

Until July 2013 lone parents were able to claim mean-tested Domestic Purposes Benefit for Sole Parents until their youngest child turned 18. A part-time and later full-time work tests existed for lone parents with a youngest child aged 14 years and over in the late 1990s and early 2000s, but the work test was removed in 2003. With the removal of the work test a requirement to develop a formal Personal Development and Employment Plan, which included work preparation and work-related activity, was introduced for all lone parents. From 2008, these plans were no longer administered as a blanket requirement, but lone parents were able to volunteer for them and only a quarter of lone parents had such a plan. However, in September 2010, a part-time work obligation was re-introduced for lone parents with a youngest dependent child aged six or older. As part of wider reforms to the welfare system in July 2013, the main lone parent income support became Sole Parent Support. Sole Parent Support can be claimed by lone parents with a youngest child under 14 and a part-time work obligation exists for those with a youngest child aged above five. Lone parents with a youngest child aged 14 and over can claim the main unemployment benefit Jobseeker Support, where full-time work obligations apply. The "investment approach" introduced in 2012 (see Section "An investment approach to participation") also required the public employment service **Work and Income** to target its employment interventions to where they are most likely to reduce long-term benefit dependency and welfare costs, which resulted in a special focus of the employment service on lone parents. The changes since 2010 resulted in a reduction of lone parents claiming income support and in an increase in lone parent employment (see Figure 1.9, Panel B). Recent employment growth is mainly driven by a rise in part-time employment, as lone parents and others on low incomes have little incentive to work more than 20 hours a week, due to high marginal effective tax rates for those working more than 20 hours (Carey, 2015).

United Kingdom

The United Kingdom introduced a work-test for lone parents in 2008, as earlier reforms – including i) a voluntary programme, which offered work-search counselling; ii) mandatory work focussed interviews with employment advisers at 6 or 12 months intervals; and iii) an in-work bonus in the first 12 months of employment – did not result in an increase of lone-parent employment rates to the desired extent. Between the end of 2008 and 2010 the applicable age of the youngest child when the work test applied was lowered from 15 to 7 years in three phases. In 2012, the age limit was further lowered, applying to lone parents with a youngest child aged 5 and over. Lone parents benefit from some exemptions such as being only available during normal school hours (until the youngest child turns 13), or taking up a job only within one month if there are difficulties in arranging childcare earlier. Since April 2014, lone parents with a youngest child aged 3 or 4 years have to engage in "work-related activity". This could include preparation of a CV, exploring the local labour market or attending training courses to improve work-related skills, but parents will not be required to apply for or take up a job as part of work-related activity.

Between 2010 and 2014, the lone-mother employment rate increased by nearly 7 percentage points (see Figure 1.9, Panel B). However, Avram et al. (2016) show that while the introduction of the work test increased flows of lone parents into work, it also resulted in a large proportion of lone parents with an existing income support entitlement to move onto health-related benefits or into non-claimant unemployment. The job quality of lone parents leaving welfare often is low. Lone parents who had worked since leaving income support were most likely to work part-time in elementary, personal service or sales and customer-service occupations and the majority were paid at around the national minimum wage or even below. Employment advisers in the public employment service or at contracted providers have no incentives to help lone parents find work of 16 or more hours, as this is the point when income support stops and lone parents become eligible for working tax credits (OECD, 2014a). Furthermore, lone parents facing additional expenditure on childcare often have no incentive to work more than 16 hours, as they may face marginal effective tax rates close to and even above 100% (Pareliussen, 2013).

Box 3.9. Recent reforms to lone parent employment policies in New Zealand, the United Kingdom and Ireland *(cont.)*

Ireland

Until July 2015, means-tested One-Parent Family Payment was available to all lone parents with a youngest child under 18 years (or 22 years if they were in full-time education). In July 2015, the age limit for the youngest child has been reduced to seven for most lone parents (e.g. recently bereaved and those with special care responsibilities are exempted). However, a work test only applies once the youngest child turns 14. At this point lone parents claiming means-tested income support can only claim Jobseeker's Allowance and must be available for full-time work. Lone parents with a youngest child aged between seven and 13 can claim the means-tested Jobseeker's Transitional payment. This transitional benefit provides work-preparation support, but does not apply a work test. In comparison to regular Jobseeker's Allowance, the Jobseeker's Transitional payment offers i) a more generous earnings disregard and taper rate for earnings above the disregard, ii) the option to work part-time for up to 5 days per week and still receive income support (subject to the means test), iii) and the possibility to take part in a course of education for those eligible for a student maintenance grant.

Childcare is often an employment barrier for mothers wanting to work, especially in Ireland where the out-of-pocket childcare costs for a lone parent are among the OECD's highest (Table 3.1). A new measure – the After-School Child Care Scheme – aims to address this. The scheme supports low-income families who find employment, increase their employment or take up a place on an employment support scheme through providing subsidised after-school childcare places for children of primary school age (4-13 years). Individuals who get a place on the scheme are entitled to a total of 52 weeks of after-school childcare (regardless of the number of children) at a cost of only EUR 15 per week. To cover childcare during school holidays the scheme funds up to ten weeks of full-time care at the same price.

Source: Avram, S.; M. Brewer and A. Salvatori (2016), "Can't Work or Won't Work: Quasi-Experimental Evidence on Work Search Requirements for Single Parents", *IZA Discussion Paper Series*, No. 10106, Bonn, http://ftp.iza.org/dp10106.pdf; Carey, D. (2015), "Making New Zealand's Economic Growth More Inclusive", *OECD Economics Department Working Papers*, No. 1256, OECD Publishing, Paris, http://dx.doi.org/10.1787/5jrw21ntclwc-en; Department of Social Protection of Ireland (2016), "One Parent Family Payment", www.welfare.ie/en/Pages/278_One-Parent-Family-Payment.aspx (accessed on 15 November 2016); Department of Social Protection of Ireland (2016), "After-school Child Care Scheme", www.welfare.ie/en/Pages/After-school-Child-Care-Scheme.aspx (accessed on 15 November 2016); New Zealand Ministry of Social Development (2013), "The Impact of the Future Focus Work Obligations for Sole Parents: Technical Report", Knowledge and Insights, Ministry of Social Development, Wellington; OECD (2014), *Connecting People with Jobs: Activation Policies in the United Kingdom*, OECD Publishing, Paris, http://dx.doi.org/10.1787/9789264217188-en; and Pareliussen, J.K. (2013), "Work Incentives and Universal Credit: Reform of the Benefit System in the United Kingdom", *OECD Economics Department Working Papers*, No. 1033, OECD Publishing, Paris, http://dx.doi.org/10.1787/5k49lcn89rkf-en.

In contrast, Denmark achieves a high rate of full-time employment among lone parents through its comprehensive system of childcare and early education services, with public expenditure for these services being the OECD's highest (*OECD Family Database*, www.oecd.org/social/family/database.htm). Parents pay a maximum of 25% of the gross operating costs for day-care services and there is no charge for low-income families. Lone parents are further supported through higher payment rates of the non means-tested child benefit than couple families (Box 3.10). In comparison to Denmark, lone parent employment rates are lower in Germany and a much higher proportion of lone parents work part-time (Table 3.1). With around 12% of claimants of the means-tested basic jobseekers allowance being lone parents, German policy makers on various levels started to pay more attention to these families over recent years. Mainstream employment services are not enough to help lone parents into employment. Their successful activation often requires more comprehensive support, including additional counselling, career guidance and (vocational) training as well as support to find solutions to reconcile work and childcare. As such comprehensive support usually goes beyond the means of employment services, Germany started to build effective support networks for lone parents (Box 3.10).

Box 3.10. Policies in Denmark and Germany to raise lone parent labour market participation

Denmark: Combining an active stance towards all parents with a well-developed childcare system and extra child benefits for lone parents

Denmark's labour market policy has pursued a strong activation stance since the 1990s, which also applies to all parents, whether partnered or single. A work test for mothers generally applies once the youngest child turns one, after the end of parental leave, although some discretionary exceptions may be granted (see Table 3.1). While net replacement rates of unemployment benefits are high, unemployment benefit eligibility criteria are strict and followed-up with consequent sanctioning of non-compliant jobseekers. Denmark also has a comprehensive system of support measures for jobseekers, reflected in the OECD's highest spending on active labour market programmes (*OECD Database on Labour Market Programmes*). Full-time employment for both single and couple parents is enabled through a comprehensive system of child benefits and childcare support. Accordingly, over three-quarters of lone mother are in employment, of which nearly 80% work full-time (see Table 3.1) and lone parent poverty rates are among the OECD's lowest (OECD, 2011).

Children below the age of 18 qualify the family for the non means-tested child and youth allowance, with payment rates depending on the number of children and their ages. The child and youth allowance is more generous for lone parent families: Lone parents receive an additional payment independent of the number of children, which is not available to couple parents and also the payments per child are higher. For a lone parent with two children (aged 4 and 6 years) the child and youth allowance is DNK 74 300 per annum, which is about 19% of the average wage in Denmark. A couple family with two children of the same age only receives DNK 27 900 (about 7% of the average wage). Notwithstanding that there are 50 weeks of paid maternity (18 weeks) and paid parental (32 weeks) leave, all parents in Denmark are already guaranteed a place in day-care when their child is 26 weeks old until they turn six (when they reach compulsory school age). Childcare subsidies are available to all households with young children in day-care. Parents pay a maximum of 25% of the gross operating expenditure for day-care services and there is no charge for low-income families. Hence, the out-of-pocket childcare cost for a lone parent with two children (aged 2 and 3) in full-time care who earns 50% of the average wage is zero. The costs are 3% of the family net income for lone parents earning 67% of the average wage and 8% for those earning the average wage. Consequently, also the proportion of children in formal childcare is very high. In 2011, 19% of children under the age of one attended formal childcare, 91% of children aged 1-2 years and 97% of children aged 3-5 years.

Germany: Encouraging the development of effective employment support for lone parents

Lone parents are an important client group for Germany's unemployment benefit system, as 9% of registered jobseekers are lone parents. The vast majority of them (92%) claim means-tested basic jobseekers allowance (unemployment benefit II), with the remainder claiming contributory unemployment insurance (unemployment benefit I). Since the introduction of the means-tested basic jobseekers allowance as part of the *Hartz reforms* in 2005, expectations of non-working parents – and especially of lone parents – increased according to the principle of mutual obligations (*Fördern und Fordern*). A work test for jobseekers allowance recipients applies once the youngest child turns three, although there is some discretion for employment counsellors in applying the work test in the face of the local conditions, especially the availability of childcare. However, regulations also stipulate that responsible local bodies should give childcare places with a preference to parents who are able to work. Since 2011, the better integration of lone-parent families has also been included in the performance management process for the local job centres. The performance of local employment agencies in integrating lone parents is publicly available through the webpage www.sgb2.info, which shows performance over time and enables comparisons between different locations. To encourage the further development of effective support for lone parents, the Federal Ministry of Labour and Social Affairs has implemented the two programmes "Good work for lone parents" and "Networks for effective support for lone parents" between 2009 and 2013, which local jobcentres were able to join on a voluntary basis.

Box 3.10. **Policies in Denmark and Germany to raise lone parent labour market participation** *(cont.)*

The programme "Good work for lone parents" supported projects by local jobcentres and other local agencies working with them that wanted to test new and innovative approaches to improve the labour market participation of lone parents. The main focus of the programme was the identification of key success factors for an improved personal and family situation of lone parents and their labour market activation and integration. Four critical success factors were identified: i) the need for a holistic and target group-oriented support to ensure that labour market barriers as well as personal barriers (e.g. health problems) are addressed; ii) the need for professional (re)orientation and (re)qualification, as many lone parents have been unemployed for a long time or have no prior work experience; iii) the importance of job-brokerage and working with employers, also to address negative preconceptions of employers towards lone parents; and iv) the importance of identifying ways to reconcile work and childcare, which includes both identifying suitable solutions also during school holidays and after school, as well as addressing negative attitudes of lone parents towards formal childcare.

The programme "Networks for effective support for lone parents" aimed at building networks for the better labour market integration of lone parents, involving local jobcentres, chambers of commerce, employers, childcare providers and other local actors. Most new networks faced a web of inefficient and overlapping support and the challenge was to build transparent, reliable and citizen-oriented support structures. The experience of the networks showed that for an effective co-operation it is crucial to identify the right partners, win them over for an active co-operation and embed the resulting network in the existing support structures of the region. An important learning of the programme was that it takes time to develop these structures. However, such structures are the prerequisite for developing specific support services and embed those in needs-oriented "service chains". The accompanying monitoring of the programme found that most networks devoted themselves to linking up service chains and optimising interfaces. The support services they developed ranged from information brochures with all important contacts to formal co-operation agreements between relevant stakeholders.

Source: Broens, K. et al. (2013), "Programmbegleitung 'Gute Arbeit für Alleinerziehende'" [Programme support 'Good work for lone parents']", Bundesministerium für Arbeit und Soziales, http://gute-arbeit-alleinerziehende.de/; Federal Employment Agency of Germany [Bundesagentur für Arbeit] (2016), "Strukturen der Arbeitslosigkeit und Hilfebedürftigkeit von Alleinerziehenden [Structures of unemployment and the need for assistance of lone parents]", June, https://statistik.arbeitsagentur.de/Navigation/Statistik/Statistik-nach-Themen/Grundsicherung-fuer-Arbeitsuchende-SGBII/Personengruppen-Bedarfsgemeinschaften/Personengruppen-Bedarfsgemeinschaften-Nav.html; Federal Ministry of Labour and Social Affairs [Bundesministerium für Arbeit un Soziales] (2013), "Alleinerziehende unterstützen – Fachkräfte gewinnen [Supporting lone parents – attracting skilled workers]", www.bmas.de/DE/Service/Medien/Publikationen/a858-alleinerziehende.html; OECD (2011), *Doing Better for Families*, OECD Publishing, Paris, http://dx.doi.org/10.1787/9789264098732-en; OECD (2014), "Denmark 2014", Country specific information for the OECD series *Benefits and Wages* www.oecd.org/els/social/workincentives.

Activation and labour market policies towards parents more generally and experiences of recent reforms of lone parent policies in other OECD countries provide useful insights for Australia:

- The **timing and scope of reforms** are fundamental factors when designing future policies and need to be thoroughly reviewed. The magnitude of increases in lone parent labour market participation in the United Kingdom is likely to be driven by the fact that reforms covered both existing and new income support recipients. The United Kingdom also deserves credit for continuing with its reforms to activate lone parents in the midst of the recession. Any possible future reforms for lone parents in Australia should cover both existing and new claimants.
- In comparison to other OECD countries, Australia's **work test** for lone parents still appears not very far-reaching. Changes to participation requirements could include introducing full-time work requirements for principle carer parents with older children or introducing a work test for principle carers earlier on.

- It is too early to assess the introduction of **mandatory work-preparation measures** for lone parents with younger children in Ireland and the United Kingdom. These measures, however, deserve further attention and something similar could be piloted in Australia for principle carer parents with children under age six, using the new *Try, Test and Learn Fund*. This would require reviewing how voluntary *jobactive* participants could receive additional services.
- In New Zealand, increased **employment services support** for lone parents is achieved through requiring the PES to target lone parents. In Germany, the labour market integration of lone parents is monitored through the performance management system of local PES offices. This in turn gives local offices an incentive to participate in programmes like the ones mentioned in Box 3.10. These findings are not easily transferrable to the Australian context, where the contracted employment service providers are free to decide on the intensity of support given to different types of clients. Hence, it will be important to review whether it is profitable for providers to provide comprehensive support to lone parents, especially when they face multiple barriers to employment as many lone parents do (see Chapter 2).
- Access to affordable, high quality **childcare** backs up Denmark's strict approach to activation, as it enables parental labour market participation. Also Germany presses ahead with increasing labour market participation of mothers with young children and more comprehensive childcare support especially for lone parents was an option under consideration. Furthermore, the German PES has a special focus on lone parents and the need to provide support (including help with childcare) beyond the usual mainstream employment services is recognised as an essential means to better integrate lone parents into the labour market.

A recently commenced programme in ten Australian local government areas called *ParentsNext* aims to address some of these issues through assisting parents to plan and prepare for employment by the time their youngest child reaches school age. Parents with children under age six and who had no paid employment in the last six months can participate on a voluntary basis, but for some recipients of Parenting Payment participation is mandatory. ParentsNext is delivered through contracted providers, some of which also deliver jobactive services. Participating parents are required to attend six-monthly appointments with their provider, to sign a Participation Plan and to participate in activities that help them prepare for employment (e.g. participation in education and training measures, improving interpersonal or presentation skills, attending health-related appointments or activities, finding out about childcare fee assistance).

Increasing labour force participation more generally

In Australia, as also in other OECD countries, many groups outside the labour market or with a weak labour market attachment are not claiming benefits and are therefore not within easy reach of employment and related services. These groups for example include inactive spouses, youths at home, people with mental health conditions, disconnected welfare leavers etc. A wide range of measures may be needed to engage with these subgroups or identify their disadvantages: new benefit entitlements (e.g. assistance benefits for youths living with their parents, disability living allowances); attractive service offers (e.g. free childcare, education, health care, or employment services); individualised taxation (or individualised benefit entitlements) that tend to bring both members of a couple into employment; or data matching to target disengaged youth for social worker visits. This section reviews a number of population groups with unmet labour market participation potential and who are not usually within reach of Australia's mainstream employment and related services.

Improving labour market and educational outcomes for disadvantaged youth

In an OECD-wide comparison Australia performs well in terms of education and labour market outcomes for young people. The youth employment rate has consistently been above the OECD average over the past 30 years and the proportion of Australian youth not in employment, education or training (NEET) is below the OECD average. However, just like in other OECD countries, disadvantaged youth often struggle and special attention is needed to assure these youth successfully transition into higher education and employment. Policy intervention needs a dual focus: to ensure that youth stay in school and complete education and to help them access the labour market.

Australia has a long tradition of delivering services for disadvantaged youth and this has been recognised in various OECD reports. However, in some instances there has been a lack of continuity of funding, even where programmes have shown good results. The *Youth Connections* programme which provided a safety net for disengaged youth through individual case management and helped reconnect them with education but was phased out nevertheless towards the end of 2014 is a good example (OECD, 2016a).

The Australian Government has filled this gap through its *Youth Employment Strategy* (2015-16 budget) which includes measures to assist young people to enter the workforce as well as improve their education levels. Two of the measures, *Transition to Work* and *Empowering YOUth Initiatives*, are worth mentioning even though at this stage it is too early to assess their impact. Both measures are focused on improving work readiness and have employment as an ultimate goal, recognising that for many disengaged youth education may not necessarily be the best way forward. Transition to Work provides intensive pre-employment assistance to young people who have disengaged and are at risk of long-term welfare dependence. The service commenced in early 2016 and is provided by 43 contracted providers in selected locations across Australia, and it includes apprenticeships and traineeships. Empowering YOUth Initiatives support new and innovative approaches to help young unemployed. Funding is available for around 40 initiatives for a maximum of two years each and includes an evaluation component.

Another initiative in Australia is the *Youth Jobs PaTH* (2016-17 budget), part of the Youth Employment Package. Youth Jobs PaTH includes three elements: employability skills training to help young jobseekers understand what employers expect and equip them with the necessary skills ("Prepare"); internships in real workplaces ("Trial"); and a Youth Bonus wage subsidy to help businesses hire young jobseekers ("Hire").

While Australia has introduced a range of new programmes and initiatives to help unemployed disadvantaged youth in their transition into the labour market, still more can be done to prevent youth unemployment and ensure school completion. Overall, the Australian education system performs well and the share of young adults with below upper secondary education is below the OECD average. But other countries have interesting initiatives in place to prevent school leaving and to assure good education outcomes of early school leavers. The Australian Curriculum, Assessment and Reporting Authority tightly monitors school performance, including attendance and test scores, but this information is not systematically shared with external specialised services that could help youth at risk of dropping out from school. OECD (2016a) therefore recommends that data on school attendance for youth should be shared with the benefit and local service administrations whenever needed. These services in turn should contact youth and their families to identify any obstacles to school attendance and offer them counselling or alternative learning options. Since 2007, the Netherlands also tightly monitors school attendance and uses this information in a number of measures to prevent early school leaving. Early results of this Dutch programme are very promising, as the number of early school leavers has been nearly halved between 2005-06 and 2012-13 (Box 3.11).

Box 3.11. **Preventing early school leaving in the Netherlands**

Since 2007, the Netherlands has introduced several measures to curb early school leaving. All young people in education receive an "education number" to facilitate the tracking of early school leaving. In line with this move, a national digital School Absenteeism Desk has been put in place. Schools report to the desk absenteeism (defined as missing 16 hours within four consecutive school weeks) and early school leaving (defined as leaving school before having acquired a basic qualification) and since 2009, reporting to the desk is compulsory. A nationwide programme to address early school leaving aims to: i) scrutinise the transition from pre-vocational secondary to vocational education; ii) take more and better action at school (schools receive financial rewards for lowering early school leaving percentages to certain levels); iii) cater better to pupils who would rather "work with their hands"; iv) support career orientation and study choices more effectively; v) offer more attractive syllabi, that include sports and culture, to keep youth in school; vi) agree with employers basic qualification requirements for early school leavers aged 18 to 23.

The Netherlands has also set up 39 regional registration and co-ordination centres to tackle early school leaving in collaboration with schools and municipalities. Students under the age of 23 who leave school without a basic qualification fall under the responsibility of the centres. They seek to guide students back into education, possibly in combination with work, in order to obtain a basic qualification. If education is no longer a feasible option, the centres help their wards find a sustainable job (often working with employment services).

Outcomes are promising. The number of early school leavers almost halved from over 50 000 in the school year 2005-06 to 28 000 in 2012-13, which is 2.1% of the total school population. The bulk of early leavers (79%) come from vocational education, 18% from secondary education, and the remaining 3% from adult education.

Source: OECD (2014), *Mental Health and Work: Netherlands*, OECD Publishing, Paris, http://dx.doi.org/10.1787/9789264223301-en.

Australia's youth initiatives focus primarily though not exclusively on promoting employment rather than education outcomes. Potentially this is a gap which should be filled to ensure a smooth transition from lower to upper-secondary education or to give youth who are already NEET a second chance in the education system. For example in Denmark, municipal youth guidance centres provide both counselling for young people up to the age of 25 in their critical transition from lower to upper-secondary education, and follow-up up on those who drop out of upper-secondary education (Box 3.12).

Box 3.12. Municipal youth guidance centres in Denmark

Municipal Youth Guidance Centres are responsible for i) counselling young people up to the age of 25 in their critical transition from lower- to upper-secondary education, and ii) following up on those who drop out of upper-secondary education. The centres co-operate closely with the educational institutions and the municipal job centre, for which young people are also a target group. The guidance centres have access to a database with a full overview of the education and training of each person under age 25 within the municipality who has not finished upper secondary education. This enables a quicker identification of vulnerable youth.

Guidance counsellors are responsible for preparing education plans for all pupils for the time after they complete lower-secondary school. Planning involves meeting pupils and parents and building on pupils' school records, which provide information on their achievements, interests, expectations for the future, and how they wish to develop. Planning starts several years before the end of compulsory schooling. Youth guidance counsellors assess the pupil's academic, social and personal competences in the 8th grade. Children assessed as not having the competences needed to be ready for further education must participate in an individually adapted, focused education and guidance programme in grade 8 and 9 in co-operation between the school and the guidance centre. The goal is that the pupil becomes ready to receive an upper secondary education by the end of grade 9 or 10.

The transition process between lower and upper secondary education is monitored and pupils aged 15 to 17 years old who fail to turn up for upper secondary education after compulsory school are monitored to prevent early school leaving. In case of non-attendance, the guidance counsellor has to get in touch with the parents within five days of being notified by the school and initiate action within 30 days. Counsellors are not allowed to provide treatment or therapy but can identify problems and refer pupils or parents to specialists – a social worker in case of severe social problems in the family, for example, or a psychologist in the event of mental illness.

There are 53 centres in Denmark with around 1 000 counsellors covering the 98 municipalities. The Ministry of Education has developed guidelines for a quality assurance system to be set up by each centre including figures regarding the scope, results and effects of the guidance provided, and a procedure for evaluating the services provided through user and employee surveys. Centres are also required to publish objectives, methods, planned activities and performance on the Internet.

Source: Euroguidance Denmark (2014), "Guidance in Education – The Educational Guidance System in Denmark", Danish Agency for Higher Education, Copenhagen; and OECD (2013), *Mental Health and Work: Denmark*, OECD Publishing, Paris, http://dx/doi/org/10.1787/9789264188631-en.

Comprehensive, full-time, second-chance educational programmes can be a suitable alternative for early school leavers who are unable or unwilling to return to a standard school, possibly because they have been out of school for too long or face additional barriers, such as family responsibilities or mental health conditions. These programmes combine catch-up courses in foundation skills with vocational classes, counselling and career guidance, and often enable participants to obtain an upper-secondary qualification. Second-chance programmes offer a flexible learning environment often with a residential component that is well adapted to early school leavers' needs and designed to help them back into education. Probably the largest residential second-chance programme is the *US Job Corps*, which has been operating since 1964. It targets disadvantaged youth up to age 24 and includes academic tuition, vocational training, counselling, social skills training, job placements and also health care (OECD, 2016e). In Australia a smaller-scale second-chance programme is offered through the so-called *youth foyers*, of which there are currently 14 across the country (OECD, 2016a). Since youth foyers are expensive to build and operate, they are likely to remain tightly targeted at a small number of youth who are committed to participating in a specific educational programme, and who lack housing. Another option to offer second-chance educational programmes for youth is to use existing education and training structures. This is done in Sweden through the *Folk High Schools*, which mainly serve adults with previous work experience. However, Folk High Schools also admit young people aged 18 and over and they may also accept those under age 18, if their municipality funds their tuition (Box 3.13).

Box 3.13. A second chance at the Folk High Schools in Sweden

Folk high schools offer a programme equal to education provided by the upper secondary schools from the age of 18. There are over 150 schools in Sweden, and the concept dates back to the 19th century. Around two-thirds of folk high schools are run by the civic society. Folk high schools are not bound by national curricula. They provide a mixture of intense counselling, coaching in social and life skills and formal education. This seems to be successful for those most remote from the school system. Schools are characterised by process-oriented pedagogy with active participation by the students e.g. in the form of theme and project work in small groups.

As mainly adults apply to folk high schools, considerable weight is placed on their previous experience, and tuition is decidedly tailored to the individual. Folk high schools are financed through funding grants from the state, county councils and municipalities. Anyone over age 18 can join and those under 18 may be admitted as long as their municipality funds their tuition.

Characteristics of the Swedish folk high schools include:

- Very low teacher-to-student ratios which allows the development of closer relationships;
- A significant share of folk high schools also offer boarding for students;
- A grading system that takes account of academic performance as well as social skills.

A major advantage of the folk high school system is that its alternative grading system does not block off the option to proceed to tertiary-level education. Instead, there is a quota in public universities reserved for graduates from folk high schools. This is likely to motivate students to graduate from the programme, as they have a realistic chance to continue onto university or higher level VET courses.

Source: OECD (2016), *Investing in Youth: Sweden*, Investing in Youth, OECD Publishing, Paris, http://dx.doi.org/10.1787/9789264267701-en.

Improving labour market outcomes of those with mental health conditions

Across the OECD, mental illness is increasingly recognised as one of the biggest obstacles and barriers to labour market participation and employment and one of the main causes of unemployment and inactivity (OECD, 2012b; OECD, 2015e). The reasons are manifold and include:

- The high prevalence of mental illness, with 20% of the working-age population reporting mental ill-health at any moment in time and up to 50% in a lifetime.
- The young age at onset of mental illness, with a median age of onset across all types of mental illness around age 14 and as low as age 11 for anxiety disorders.
- The high stigma and self-stigma coming with mental illness, resulting in high rates of under-treatment and non-disclosure and neglect by all stakeholders.

The problem is only recognised recently and therefore no OECD country has markedly better employment outcomes for this population group; employment rates for people with mental illness tend to be highest in countries with high overall employment rates. However, the gap in the employment rate between people with and without a mental illness is somewhat larger in Australia than in other countries for which comparable data are available: the employment gap is 14 and 34 percentage points for Australians with mild-to-moderate and more severe mental illness, respectively.

Australia belongs to the OECD countries in which the awareness of mental illness as a barrier to employment is quite high and the degree of stigma attached potentially lower. This is reflected in a range of good-practice programmes available in Australia targeted to young people and aimed at improving their mental well-being (OECD, 2015e; OECD, 2015f). This includes i) *Kidsmatter* and *Mindmatters*, two health promotion programmes developed for primary and secondary schools, respectively; ii) *Headspace*, a special entity with over 100 centres across the country providing easily accessible, low-threshold services for young people with mental illness aged 12-25; and iii) the previous *Youth Connections* and the new *Transition to Work* programme (both mentioned in the previous section) which aim at reconnecting disengaged young people with education, training and employment. These initiatives are extremely important in view of the early onset of mental illness which often results in early school leaving and poorer education outcomes and, thereby, much poorer employment opportunities and transitions.

Australia has also taken a number of steps to close the large treatment gap. It has i) successfully expanded access to mental health care through its *Access to Allied Psychological Services* initiative, which commenced in 2003; ii) improved the mental health knowledge of general practitioners through extensive training courses which 90% of all general practitioners have completed: and iii) promoted the engagement of mental health nurses in the primary care treatment process through the *Mental Health Nurse Incentive Programme* to improve treatment compliance and the continuity of care.

These initiative and programmes will eventually contribute to better treatment of mental illness and higher participation in the labour market by people with mental illness. However, there are other policy areas in the *mental health and work* field which Australia could put larger focus on. The OECD Council Recommendation on Integrated Mental Health, Skills and Work Policy (OECD, 2016g) has identified four settings in which major progress will have to be made: youth policy; health policy; workplace policy; and employment/welfare policy. In the latter two areas, much more could be done in Australia to promote better employment outcomes for people with mental illness.

In Australia it is largely left to employers to address workplace risks and sickness and return to work matters although the workers' compensation system provides a strong financial incentive to reduce *work-related* health and safety risks and encourage rehabilitation and return to work following work-related injuries and illnesses, including mental illnesses (see also the section on disability policy). Several OECD countries have recently strengthened their work environment legislation in order to promote working conditions that are conducive to good mental health. It is important in this regard to also include in such legislation more concrete guidelines for employers on what to do and stronger monitoring of employer obligations and actions. Belgium and Denmark have both done so in different ways, thereby providing models to follow for Australian workplace legislation (Box 3.14). The examples also demonstrate how difficult it is to implement such legislation in an effective manner.

Securing working conditions that are conducive to mental health is only one side of the coin. Many workers experience mental health conditions which are not necessarily related to the workplace or the specific working conditions. In many cases these issues have significant repercussions on the worker's performance and productivity (OECD, 2012b; OECD, 2015e). It is therefore important to address these issues also in a workplace context. Performance losses are costly for employers who therefore should have an intrinsic interest to tackle underlying problems. But employers are often unaware of their workers' mental illnesses due to both non-disclosure and significant stigma related to such issues but also significant unawareness among workers themselves.

Box 3.14. **Strengthening legislation in Belgium and Denmark to assess and prevent work environment risks**

Denmark's working environment legislation

Workplace health and safety in Denmark is regulated in the Working Environment Act, through agreements between the social partners and overseen by the Working Environment Authority (WEA). Legal provisions require employers to manage psychosocial work environment (PWE) risks in the workplace. Since 2007, the WEA has been responsible for inspecting the PWE in all enterprises. It is a big shift from the more traditional health and safety focus of the WEA and has prompted it to develop an inspection strategy. The WEA has developed 24 sector- and job-specific guidance tools. Each guidance tool describes the prevalence of risk factors and the potential resources of a company to prevent problems – the aim being for each company to seek a balance between risks and prevention resources. The tool also describes the possible consequences of an imbalance between risks and resources, such as bad reputation, loss of commitment, long delays, complaint from customers, high staff turnover rates, or long-term sickness absence rates.

WEA inspectors have been trained in how to use the guidance tools and how to assess and evaluate the PWE health and safety risks. The job of inspecting PWE risks has been facilitated through method descriptions and instructions, by templates on how to prepare improvement notices (in case improvements are needed), and through the sharing of best-practice examples. A full impact assessment of the WEA strategy and the guidance tools has not yet been carried out. However, preliminary results from focus group interviews with inspectors suggest that the guidance tools are used widely before, during, and after inspections and that employers consider them very useful. Although the number of improvement notices in relation to PWE problems has increased, they still comprise only 5% of all notices issued by the WEA in relation to health and safety aspects.

Belgium's legislation on well-being at work

In Belgium, employers are legally obliged to take necessary preventive measures to preserve the well-being of their employees. Employers must carry out risk assessments to identify situations and risk factors at the workplace that can generate psychosocial distress. On the basis of such an assessment, the employer must draw up a five-year global prevention plan and an annual action plan to avoid distress at work and limit its consequences. The risk analyses and prevention and action plans are conducted in collaboration with prevention advisors and employee representatives. Employers have to appoint a prevention advisor to assist them in implementing the risk prevention policy. For companies with up to 50 employees, the prevention advisor must be from an external provider to avoid conflicts of interest. These external services employ both occupational doctors and prevention advisors who are specialised in one or more of the following five fields: safety at work, occupational medicine, ergonomics, occupational hygiene, and psychosocial aspects of work.

An evaluation has revealed that the practical implementation of the legislation on well-being at work remains deficient. First, employers too seldom carry out psychosocial risk analyses, chiefly because of the high cost involved and the resistance of employers who fear a negative analysis and the implications it may have on the organisation of work. Second, many employers are not aware of their legal obligations and the importance and advantages of prevention policies. Third, on the side of the employees, there is a lack of awareness of the role and existence of the prevention advisors. Finally, prevention advisors have little to no time for the prevention of psychosocial risks in the workplace as they are fully occupied with individual complaints of harassment at work. Because of the lack of financial incentives for employers to adapt the work and workplace, some are unwilling to co-operate, which discourages occupational health specialists from specialising in the field psychosocial risk prevention – less than 5% of prevention advisors are specialised in this field.

Source: OECD (2013), *Mental Health and Work: Denmark*, OECD Publishing, Paris, http://dx.doi.org/10.1787/9789264188631-en; Senior Labour Inspectors Committee (2008), "Report on the Evaluation of the Danish Working Environment Authority in 2008", Copenhagen; OECD (2013), *Mental Health and Work: Belgium*, OECD Publishing, Paris, http://dx.doi.org/10.1787/9789264187566-en; and Service public fédéral Emploi, Travail et Concertation sociale (2011), "Évaluation de la législation relative à la prévention de la charge psychosociale occasionnée par le travail, dont la violence et le harcèlement moral ou sexuel au travail", Brussels.

Where mental health conditions are *work-related*, some countries, including Australia, have in place strong financial incentives to address such matters through their workers' compensation systems. The high costs resulting for employers from such cases explain to a certain degree why the prevalence of such problems has declined in most OECD countries and why the workers' compensation system is quite successful in keeping workers in their jobs, also in Australia. Where mental health conditions are not work-related, there may be a need for additional incentives for employers to take action to prevent labour market exit and facilitate job retention, especially also in Australia. The Netherlands is the country that has gone furthest in shifting the costs of *general* (not work-related) sickness and disability onto employers, with the agreement of the social partners and significant success. Dutch policy is at first sight not easily transferable but the lessons learned should be kept in mind: employer incentives matter and can change individual behaviour drastically, especially if they are matched with complementary obligations and incentives for the affected workers (Box 3.15).

Box 3.15. **Significant financial incentives for employers and workers in the Netherlands have lowered sickness absences and disability benefit claims considerably**

In the Netherlands, several policy changes have been introduced to compel employers (and workers) to face up to their responsibility in sickness matters. The Reduced Absenteeism Act (1994), the 2004 revision of the 1996 Wage Payment during Sickness Act, and the Gatekeeper Improvement Act (2002) have contributed to significant improvements in sickness management. When a worker becomes sick, the employer is obliged to continue paying 70%-100% of the salary for two years during which the worker is protected by law against lay-off. Moreover, employers are required to hire a case manager to oversee the return-to-work process. Within six weeks of going off sick, employees must visit an occupational physician who is paid by the employer. Within eight weeks, employer and employee are obliged to agree on an action plan, which spells out the responsibilities of both sides in ensuring a quick return to work. The employer is responsible for monitoring the return-to-work process every six weeks and for recording all actions undertaken. Both employer and employee may be sanctioned for not collaborating in the return-to-work process, which is assessed by the Employee Insurance Agency after two years of sickness absence. If an employer cannot adjust a job to enable a sick worker to return to work, both are obliged to look for suitable work for the worker in another company. Occupational health services, reintegration offices, and employer branch organisations can facilitate the new job search.

The sickness absence rate in the Netherlands has fallen sharply in the past 15 years and is now close to the OECD average. Yet it remains high among people suffering from mental ill-health. Moreover, not all employers live up to their responsibilities in return-to-work management. For example, every second employer has no guideline on when to contact an occupational physician in case of sickness absence. Employer sanctions are frequent: in one in five sickness absences longer than two years employers fail to meet their obligations and, as a sanction, have to continue sick pay at the same level for a third year.

Source: De Jong, P., T. Everhardt and C. Schrijvershof (2011), *Toepassing van de wet Verbetering Poortwachter* [Application of the Gatekeeper Improvement Act], APE, Den Haag; Koopmans, P., C. Roelen, and J. Groothoff (2008), "Frequent and Long-term Absence as a Risk Factor for Work Disability and Job Termination Among Employees in the Private Sector", *Occupational and Environmental Medicine*, Vol. 65, pp. 494-499; and OECD (2014), *Mental Health and Work: Netherlands*, OECD Publishing, Paris, http://dx.doi.org/10.1787/9789264223301-en.

Employment and social policy in Australia could also do more to help people with mental illness stay in and return to the labour market. For example, it is important that the employment system and the employment service providers identify mental illness of jobseekers early on to prevent long-term unemployment and the sliding into disability benefit dependence. Australia uses a strong instrument at intake into the benefit system, the Job Seekers Classification Instrument (see Box 3.2), but misses an opportunity in this process to also measure mental illness-related barriers to reintegration systematically. If mental health-related barriers were known, the next step would be an efficient co-operation between employment services and the mental health sector and the integration of health and employment support. This is crucial for the labour market reintegration of jobseekers with mental illness because waiting for the health issue to be solved is counterproductive and keeping people away from work for too long; many of these problems are chronic and cannot be fully healed in. Until today, only few OECD countries have taken concrete steps to better identify mental illness-related barriers of jobseekers and provide better integrated, simultaneously delivered employment and health support but some promising initiatives exist (Arends et al., 2014; OECD, 2015e). Belgium is a country in which the public employment service has taken important steps in this direction, at least to a certain degree (Box 3.16).

The Recommendation of the OECD Council on Integrated Mental Health, Skills and Work Policy has a very strong focus on integrated policies and services in a range of policy arenas as the main government response to better support the large number of people with mental illness and improve their employment outcomes. Australia is well placed to make important inroads in this direction.

Box 3.16. Assessing mental health conditions early and providing integrated health and employment support in Belgium

Assessing mental health conditions at unemployment intake

Since 2010, newly unemployed jobseekers are systematically assessed by the Flemish Public Employment Service (VDAB) for problems that hinder their re-employment. The target group includes people with reduced psychological stability or unable to deal with stress. Upon intake, caseworkers use an assessment form to map jobseekers' possibilities and inabilities. Caseworkers look out for employment-specific competencies and qualifications, job-search behaviour, communication and social skills, disabilities and health problems. After the caseworker has completed the assessment form and proposed a follow-up programme, a VDAB psychologist has to approve the application. The aim of the assessment is to quickly detect multiple problems in order to prevent long-term unemployment and offer the jobseeker a tailor-made activation programme. Assessment can be requested at any time during unemployment if there is any sign of a problem. When a caseworker believes there is a more severe mental health condition, he can refer the client for a diagnosis to a VDAB psychologist or an external specialist in in-depth multidisciplinary screening.

In the first half of 2014, 7 676 jobseekers were registered for an assessment by the VDAB. Of those 8% were referred for in-depth multidisciplinary screening. After following an activation programme, 35% were ready to work on the regular labour market. The rest need additional support and care. Supervisors of the activation programmes are satisfied with the quality of the screening reports they receive from caseworkers. The reports contain sufficient information on jobseeker' possibilities and inabilities. The assessment form is easily accessible and leaves plenty of scope for information sharing. However, supervisors believe the screening process could be improved by adding objective facts about jobseekers, in addition to self-assessment.

Providing integrated health and employment support

In 2009, the VDAB in Belgium developed a project in co-operation with the mental health and welfare sectors designed for jobseekers with severe mental, psychological, or psychiatric problems. Under the scheme, they follow intensive activation programmes that combine care and employment support provided by a specialised non-profit centre. All services are financed by the Flemish Government and free of charge for jobseekers. The activation team consists of three players: a job coach; a health coach; and an empowerment coach. VDAB pays a fixed amount to each coach and requires them to work closely together in activation guidance and to meet on a regular basis.

Box 3.16. Assessing mental health conditions early and providing integrated health and employment support in Belgium *(cont.)*

The job coach, employed by the centre, puts in place an individual action plan together with the jobseeker and introduces him to the health coach and the empowerment coach who are responsible for identifying the right services in the health sector and welfare sector respectively. During the entire process, the job coach makes sure that the activation guidance keeps its focus firmly on work. The health coach, typically a psychologist working in a centre for mental health, focuses on the health issues and provides rehabilitation and training in, for instance, self-confidence or coping with stress. The empowerment coach from the welfare sector focuses on economic, psychosocial and social impediments and deals with issues such as mobility, personal budgeting, and housing.

Co-operation between the three sectors delivers tailored services to long-term jobseekers far away from the labour market. Co-operation with a psychologist, the focus on case management, and the multidisciplinary team meetings are the major strengths of the programme. In 2011, some 12% of the long-term unemployed in Flanders underwent in-depth multidisciplinary screening. Between 2007 and 2012, 11% of participants in the activation guidance programme found a job in the regular labour market and no longer receive unemployment benefits. Another 5.5% moved into sheltered employment and 2.8% into other forms of employment outside the regular labour market.

Source: OECD (2013), *Mental Health and Work: Belgium*, OECD Publishing, Paris, http://dx.doi.org/10.1787/9789264187566-en.

Increasing female labour market participation more generally

Female labour market participation still varies to a considerable degree across OECD countries because of large differences in a number of critical factors, including both individual characteristics and the institutional and policy set-up in a country (Box 3.17). It is important to understand the features and analyse the effectiveness of policy measures aimed at favouring women's labour market participation in those OECD countries that have the lowest gender employment gaps. Eurofound (2016) provides a useful classification of such policy measures, organising them into i) labour market policy measures (i.e. ALMPs, tax-benefit policies), ii) childcare support measures (i.e. direct or indirect support with the costs and provision of childcare), iii) leave policies (i.e. maternity and parental leave), and iv) flexible working policies (e.g. availability of part-time employment and reduced working hours). A detailed analysis of such policies goes beyond the remit of this report. While a number of labour market policy measures were already covered in the section on lone parents, this section briefly discusses childcare support measures and flexible working policies, while a discussion of parental leave policies is not included in this report.

There is wide variation in the prevalence of different forms of public childcare support across the OECD, including cash benefits (e.g. childcare subsidies), public in-kind services (e.g. public provision of childcare and out-of-school-hours care) and fiscal support (e.g. tax advantages for formal childcare). In Australia, public spending on family benefits is concentrated on cash payments (OECD, 2016h). Assistance with the costs of early childhood education and care (ECEC) is provided via means-tested fee subsidies (through Child Care Benefit and Jobs, Education and Training Child Care Fee Assistance) and the not means-tested Child Care Rebate. In response to the Productivity Commission's report on Childcare and Early Childhood Learning, the Budget Review 2016-17 announced to replace these benefits with a single means-tested Child Care Subsidy from July 2018 (Productivity Commission, 2014). The new subsidy will cover 50%-85% of a families' childcare fees up to an hourly cap and with an upper annual cap for families earning more than AUD 185 000. Eligibility criteria include that the family satisfies an activity test, with the hours of subsidised care depending on the hours spent in work, training, study or other recognised activities such as volunteering (The Treasury, 2015b). Low-income families, who do not meet the activity test, will be subsidised for up to 24 hours of childcare each fortnight, in recognition of children from non-working families being developmentally more vulnerable and benefitting particularly from ECEC (Productivity Commission, 2014). Other Budget measures include the Child Care Safety Net programme, which will provide targeted support to disadvantaged or vulnerable families who encounter barriers to accessing regular childcare and a two-year pilot programme, which extends childcare fee assistance to in-home care provided by nannies.

Different emphasis in underlying policy objectives can help explain cross-national differences in whether governments invest in financial (cash and/or fiscal) or in-kind childcare support. For example, rather than financial support – which may often weaken the financial incentive to work and reduce female employment numbers and/or hours – countries like Denmark (see Box 3.10) and Sweden (see Box 3.18) have chosen to develop systems of universally accessible ECEC, which in turn have fostered high shares of female full-time employment. While the ECEC systems in Denmark and Sweden date back to the 1980s and earlier, ECEC reforms have been more recently introduced in Korea, France and Germany. The reforms have usually been driven by a number of policy objectives, including child development and early learning outcomes, addressing persistently low fertility rates and the desire to keep highly educated women in the labour force. The expansion of ECEC in Korea and Germany was concentrated on the expansion of public or publicly subsidised childcare settings. France, in contrast, has concentrated on providing more generous financial support for families using childminders and in-home nannies (see Box 3.18).

Flexible workplace practices (such as part-time work, flexible start and finishing times, teleworking, etc.) can also improve the work/family balance, often in a manner also consistent with enterprise needs. Workplace practices are often governed by collective agreements or informal employer rules, particularly in smaller enterprises. Australia is among the small number of OECD countries, which grant workers the right to adjust their working hours (OECD, 2011). Such rights signal the importance of work/life balance considerations to employers, while generally granting employers the right to refuse for compelling business reasons. In Australia, the *Fair Work Act* of 2009 provided employees with a legal right to request flexible working arrangements, depending on the personal and family circumstances (including the responsibility to care for a child of school age or younger). Accordingly, in 2014 almost two-thirds (64%) of all Australian working families with children 12 years and under had a parent who made use of flexible working time to help care for their children. Flexible working hours (42%) and part-time work (29%) were the most commonly used work arrangements, followed by working from home (21%) (ABS, 2015).

Box 3.17. The determinants of female labour force participation

Recent evidence shows that female labour force participation is influenced by a number of factors, such as the rise in female educational attainment, changes in the nature of the labour market, family-friendly policies, and the tax system (Thévenon, 2013 and 2015; Cipollone et al., 2013; Kalíšková, 2015). Changes in labour markets have been powerful factors in growing female labour force participation in OECD countries, particularly the development of the services sector and the expansion of part-time work, which have enabled a greater proportion of women to work and keep working after they start to have children.

Policies which aim to help parents reconcile work and family commitments are also found to have a positive influence on female labour force participation. With national data from 18 OECD countries between 1980 and 2007, Thévenon (2013, 2015) analyses how aggregate levels of female labour force participation respond to policies that support work-life balance. The analysis takes in variables on paid leave (public spending and duration), childcare services for children under the age of three (public spending and enrolment rates), public expenditure on other family benefits, and financial incentives to work (such as tax incentives that encourage both partners in couple families to go out to work). The results reveal that expansions in childcare service provisions significantly boost women's labour market participation and exert a greater positive influence on female employment than variations in the weeks of paid leave. Childcare provision for the under 3s doubled, on average, between the mid-1990s and the late 2000s, producing an estimated 2.5-percentage point increase in the employment rates of 25-54 year-old women – a quarter of the total increase between 1995 and 2008.

The effect of childcare services also differs across countries, but is most pronounced in those where support for working mothers is greatest. Accordingly, expanded provision of childcare services for the under-3s was found to have a weaker effect on female employment rates in the Continental and Southern European countries, where it may have merely converted informal into formal childcare (Akunduz and Plantenga, 2015).

The effect of policies also varies according to women's levels of educational attainment. Cipollone et al. (2015) found that childcare subsidies and child-friendly policies had positive impacts on the activity rates of 25-34 year-old women with children who were educated to medium and high levels. By contrast, there was no effect among poorly educated women.

Female employment is also responsive to financial incentives. Thévenon (2013, 2015) estimates that higher tax rates for second earners deter woman from working, although that effect is tempered in an institutional environment which is friendly to a work-life balance. The effect of financial incentives is greatest in English-speaking countries, where female employment rates appear to be reduced by increases in the duration of paid leave and/or the relative tax rates affecting second earners in couple families. This finding makes sense in countries where labour markets are flexible enough to allow workers to move in and out of the labour force, and where working hours can be adjusted to family needs and constraints like high child carecosts.

Kalíšková (2015) also measured the effect of tax-benefit policies on female labour supply in a broad sample of 26 European countries between 2005 and 2010. Model estimates suggest that a 10-percentage point increase in the "participation tax rate" – the share of lost earnings offset by lower taxes and higher benefits when a mother is not in paid work – reduces by 2 percentage points the likelihood of working. The effect is more pronounced among single mothers, women in the middle of the skills distribution, and in countries that have lower rates of female employment.

Source: OECD (2016), *Dare to Share: Germany's Experience Promoting Equal Partnership in Families*, OECD Publishing, Paris, http://dx.doi.org/10.1787/9789264259157-en.

Box 3.18. **The expansion of early childhood education and care (ECEC) in Sweden, Korea, Germany and France**

Sweden

In 1965, only about 3% of children up to the age of 6 used public childcare and preschool services in Sweden. However, rapid expansion throughout the 1970s and early 1980s had increased the provision to roughly 50% as early as 1985. Sustained public investment has seen growth in enrolment continue steadily and almost year-on-year ever since. In 2013, about 87% of all Swedish children aged 1-6 years used public ECEC services.

The expansion of ECEC in Sweden has built largely on publicly subsidised and, for the most part, publicly run centre-based services and collective care arrangements. Home-based family day care services are available, but accounted for only around 2% of children aged 0-5 in 2013 (OECD, 2015g). ECEC in Sweden has since become an integral part of the education system with its own curriculum and educational targets. However, Sweden's public, comprehensive and centre-based system is relatively expensive. In 2013, public expenditure on ECEC services was 1.64% of GDP, the second highest level of spending on ECEC in the OECD after Iceland (OECD, 2016h).

Korea

ECEC provision in Korea is, for the most part, a relatively recent development. As recently as 2002, only around 30% of children aged 0-6 years used childcare or preschool facilities. However, rapid growth in the 2000s and early 2010s saw that rate rise sharply. In 2014, more than 66% of children below 6 years of age were enrolled in some form of childcare or preschool service.

Like Sweden, the rapid growth of ECEC provision in Korea has been built almost entirely on the use of centre-based collective care arrangements. In large part, it has been driven by the scale of public financial assistance for parents using centre-based childcare. Indeed, Korea has long subsidised such costs for children from very low-income households. From 2004 onwards, however, it loosened the income criteria for the subsidy and raised the centre-based ECEC subsidy itself. In 2013, it scrapped the means test for the subsidy altogether, effectively creating a universal programme of public assistance for centre-based care, regardless of income level. As in Sweden, other forms of publicly backed care are available. In 2007, the government introduced a subsidised "personal care service", offering parents the option of individual childcare in the home. The personal care service is generally a part-time provision, but a full-time service for children aged 0 to 2 years old is available. However, the service is used by only a minority of children – less than 1% in 2014 (OECD, 2016h).

Germany

Over the past two decades, Germany has introduced a number of major reforms increasing the availability of publicly provided childcare for pre-school children, hoping - among other reasons - to encourage more mothers with young children to take up employment. The first important reform was the introduction of a legal claim to a place in kindergarten from 1996 for all pre-school children aged 3-6 years. Prior to the reform, public childcare coverage for 3- and 4-year-olds was severely rationed in West Germany. An evaluation of this reform, found that it increased employment by mothers with children aged 3-4 years by 4-6 percentage points. The reform resulted in some increase in full-time employment, but the effect was larger for part-time employment (Bauernschuster and Schlotter, 2015). Furthermore, around two-thirds of mothers use childcare for other reasons than taking up a job. These results are not surprising, given that most children attend kindergarten on a part-time basis only (OECD, 2016h). Nevertheless, a "cautious back-of-the-envelope" analysis of the costs and benefits by Bauernschuster and Schlotter suggests that about 60% of the operating expenses of public child care (net of parents' fees), are covered by increased income tax and social security contribution receipts resulting from the higher maternal employment.

Since 2005, several laws aimed at increasing subsidised childcare slots for children aged 1-3 years and since August 2013 parents have a legal right to subsidised childcare for a child aged one year or above regardless of the employment status or income of the parents. While in 2006 only 16% of children under 3 years were enrolled in formal childcare (Geyer et al., 2015), the number of available places is expected to nearly triple between 2006 and 2018 (OECD, 2016h). The number of guaranteed hours varies widely across Germany's federal states (*Länder*), with some providing part-time places only and others generally offering full-time care. With the reform still in its early days, it is too early for a comprehensive evaluation of its impact on paternal labour market participation.

Box 3.18. The expansion of early childhood education and care (ECEC) in Sweden, Korea, Germany and France *(cont.)*

Modelled estimates (e.g. by Geyer et al., 2015) point towards a significant increase in maternal labour market participation. The positive labour market impacts are, however, likely to have been subdued due to a new childcare allowance (*Betreuungsgeld*) introduced at the same time. This allowance is paid to parents with children aged 15-36 months not using publicly subsidised childcare. The idea was that these families should also benefit from care subsidies in the form of direct cash transfers. The allowance is likely to have counteracted the positive work stimulus created by the legal claim to a childcare slot (Müller and Wrohlich, 2016). In July 2015, the allowance as a federally paid benefit was, however, declared unconstitutional by Germany's Federal Constitutional Court. While not available as a benefit on the federal level, three of Germany's 16 federal states continue paying a comparable benefit on a state level.

France

France has a very long tradition of extensive ECEC provision, particularly for children aged 3-5 years. Provision for this age group is dominated by the comprehensive *école maternelle* (preschool) system – public, centre-based services that, like the Swedish preschools, are considered a core part of the national education system. Already in the early 1960s the system catered for almost two-thirds of children aged 3-5 years and since 1989, all 3-5 year-olds have been entitled to a place in the local *école maternelle*, with participation effectively at 100% ever since.

ECEC services for children under 3 years, however, are more fragmented and decentralised and the number of slots in public low-priced nurseries is much lower than demand. Public nurseries are complemented by a system of private qualified childminders and in-home nannies, whose cost are partly subsidised. Several public programmes, consisting of childcare subsidies and tax credits, alleviate the financial burden of childcare for families. Low-income households receive a base subsidy, regardless of whether or not they use formal childcare. All families that employ a qualified childminder or an in-home nanny receive an extra childcare subsidy. This subsidy is not conditional on the parents working, but it is reduced by 30% in the case of single-income couples compared to double-income couples or lone parents. Families are also exempted from a large share of the social security contributions for their childminder or nanny. In addition, all households which use paid childcare can claim a generous tax credit at the end of the financial year for their childcare expenses. As these subsidies were introduced at different times, families often faced a complex system of subsidies. To reduce this complexity, as well as increase its generosity, a single system for both allowances and social security contributions was introduced in 2004. The new PAJE (*Prestation d'accueil du Jeune Enfant* [benefit for the care of young children]) system created a streamlined system for all childcare subsidies, reduced the administrative burden for families and sharply increased the childcare subsidies. On average childcare costs decreased by 50%, with median income families benefiting most. An evaluation by Givord and Marbot (2015) found that the short-term impact of the reform on the labour force participation of French mothers appears significant but modest in size (around 1 percentage point). These results are likely to be driven by that fact that the reform partially crowded out the use of informal childcare arrangements in favour of subsidised ones. Furthermore, also prior to the reform the participation rate of French mothers with young children was already quite high compared to most other OECD countries.

Source: Bauernschuster, S. and M. Schlotter (2015), "Public Child Care and Mothers' Labor Supply: Evidence from Two Quasi-Experiments", *Journal of Public Economics*, Vol. 123, http://dx.doi.org/10.1016/j.jpubeco.2014.12.013; Geyer, J., P. Haan and K. Wrohlich (2015), "The Effects of Family Policy on Maternal Labor Supply: Combining Evidence from a Structural Model and a Quasi-experimental Approach", *Labour Economics*, Vol. 36, http://dx.doi.org/10.1016/j.labeco.2015.07.001; Givord, P. and C. Marbot (2015), "Does the Cost of Child Care Affect Female Labor Market Participation? An Evaluation of a French Reform of Childcare Subsidies", *Labour Economics*, Vol. 36, October, http://dx.doi.org/10.1016/j.labeco.2015.07.003; Müller, K.-U. and K. Wrohlich (2016), "Two Steps Forward—One Step Back? Evaluating Contradicting Child Care Policies in Germany", *CESifo Economic Studies*, Vol. 62, No. 4, http://dx.doi.org/10.1093/cesifo/ifv020; OECD (2015), *Starting Strong IV: Monitoring Quality in Early Childhood Education and Care*, OECD Publishing, Paris, http://dx.doi.org/10.1787/9789264233515-en; and OECD (2017), *Dare to Share: Germany's Experience Promoting Equal Partnership in Families*, OECD Publishing, Paris, http://dx.doi.org/10.1787/9789264259157-en.

Key findings

Australia's labour market is highly functional, employment rates are high overall in an international comparison and welfare and labour market policy in many areas contains elements that have become a benchmark for other OECD countries. However, there is room for Australia to do better because several population groups are underrepresented in the labour market today. Many of these groups face considerable employment barriers and a substantial subgroup of them even multiple barriers. Looking at policies and approaches in other countries can provide ideas on how to *i)* move forward in better utilising untapped labour resources and *ii)* maximise the gains from public investment, thereby contributing to both social cohesion and inclusive economic growth.

There is not one OECD country that could serve as a benchmark for Australia, but there are many different policy examples from many different countries that are worth exploring in more depth to inform the policy process in Australia. Some of the most relevant ideas and lessons from other OECD countries highlighted in this chapter which Australia could consider to adopt include the following:

- Early intervention and job-to-job transition support for displaced workers;
- Focus on sustainable outcomes in funding employment service providers;
- Mutual obligations for mature age jobseekers, in line with other age groups;
- Return-to-work support for workers at risk of long-term sickness absence;
- Improved sickness certificates through work-focussed certification guidelines;
- Work testing for lone parents coupled with the provision of affordable childcare;
- Help disadvantaged youth complete school and education and transition to work;
- Mental health focus in workplace legislation and employment service provision;
- Close the gender employment gap by facilitating a better work and life balance;
- Close the employment gap between Indigenous and non-Indigenous Australians.

Other OECD countries do better in some of these areas, and there is some evidence available about the effectiveness of these approaches, even though labour market policy generally suffers from a lack of rigorous evaluation and evidence. The Australian Government aims to raise the labour market participation of those groups currently underrepresented and this is indeed necessary to ensure economic growth and social cohesion in a time of rapid population ageing. Australia should make efforts towards developing better practices in all those respects, and it can do so in the context of an investment approach to welfare which it is currently experimenting with. The analysis in this report suggests that any attempt to assure a more efficient and more effective use of scarce public resources needs to be broad enough to take full account of the manifold employment barriers of those not or only weakly attached to the labour market.

Notes

1. While *age* is used in the profiling process, it is just one of 18 explanatory factors to assess a jobseekers likelihood of remaining on income support for 12 months or more.

2. Providers are expected to have monthly appointments with jobseekers under age 30 to discuss the job search they undertook in the previous months and refer jobseekers to identified jobs. For jobseekers over age 30, providers are free to decide on the frequency of appointments, apart from a mandatory comprehensive initial interview with all referred jobseekers (Department of Employment, 2014).

3. Some initial mutual obligations were already introduced in 2003. Principle carer parents with a youngest child six years or older were required to attend a compulsory annual interview with a Centrelink advisor. Those with a youngest child of 13-15 years had a participation requirement of 150 hours of approved activities such as work schemes, job search or training for every 26 weeks of receiving income support and a requirement to report activity every three months. But there was no obligation to take-up paid work.

4. Principle carer parents aged 30 years or more have a participation requirement of 200 hours (instead of the usual 390 hours) over 26 weeks, which they can meet through suitable paid work, approved study, or voluntary work. Principle carer parents aged 18-30 years have a participation requirement of 390 hours instead of the usual 650 hours for other jobseekers in this age group.

5. In Ireland, a full-time work test applies once the youngest child turns 14. In New Zealand a part-time work test applied for lone parents with a youngest child aged 5-13 and a full-time work test for those with a youngest child aged 14 and over. In the United Kingdom there are no hours specified, but once lone parents work 16 or more hours, work-search conditionality stops. Furthermore, once working 16 hours lone parents become eligible for working tax credits, giving them little incentive to work full time.

References

ABS – Australian Bureau of Statistics (2015), "Childhood Education and Care, Australia, June 2014", catalogue number 4402.0, http://www.abs.gov.au/browse?opendocument&ref=topBar.

Akunduz, Y.E and J. Plantenga (2015), "Childcare Prices and Maternal Employment: A Meta-Analysis", *Utrecht University School of Economics Discussion Paper*, No. 15-14.

Anger, C. et al. (2012), "Gesamtwirtschaftliche Effekte einer Ganztagsbetreuung von Kindern von Alleinerziehenden [Macroeconomic effects of full-day care for children of lone parents]", Cologne Institute for Economic Research, Study on behalf of the German Federal Ministry for Family Affairs, Senior Citizens, Women and Youth and the German Red Cross, Berlin.

Arends, I., et al. (2014), "Mental Health and Work: Achieving Well-integrated Policies and Service Delivery", *OECD Social, Employment and Migration Working Papers*, No. 161, OECD Publishing, Paris, http://dx.doi.org/10.1787/5jxsvvn6pq6g-en.

Arni, P. (2011): "Langzeitarbeitslosigkeit verhindern: Intensivberatung und -coaching für ältere Stellensuchende – ein Weg zu verbesserten Arbeitsmarktchancen?" ["Preventing long-term unemployment: Intensive counseling and coaching for mature age jobseekers – a path towards improved labour market opportunities?"], Office for Economy and Labour [Amt für Wirtschaft und Arbeit] of the Canton of Aargau and University of Lausanne.

Avram, S.; M. Brewer and A. Salvatori (2016), "Can't Work or Won't Work: Quasi-Experimental Evidence on Work Search Requirements for Single Parents", *IZA Discussion Paper Series*, No. 10106, Bonn, http://ftp.iza.org/dp10106.pdf.

Bauernschuster, S. and M. Schlotter (2015), "Public child care and mothers' labor supply: Evidence from two quasi-experiments", in *Journal of Public Economics*, Vol. 123, http://dx.doi.org/10.1016/j.jpubeco.2014.12.013.

Bertram, C. et al. (2014), "Work Programme Evaluation: Operation of the commissioning model, finance and programme delivery", *Department for Work and Pensions Research Report*, No. 893, London.

Bolliger, C. et al. (2012), "Eingliederung vor Rente. Evaluation der Früherfassung und der Integrationsmassnahmen in der Invalidenversicherung" [Rehabilitation Before Pension. Evaluation of Early Detection and Integration Measures in the Disability Insurance], FoP-IV Forschungsbericht, Bundesamt für Sozialversicherungen, Bern.

Broens, K. et al. (2013), "Programmbegleitung 'Gute Arbeit für Alleinerziehende' [Programme support 'Good work for lone parents']", Bundesministerium für Arbeit und Soziales, http://gute-arbeit-alleinerziehende.de/.

Carey, D. (2015), "Making New Zealand's economic growth more inclusive", *OECD Economics Department Working Papers*, No. 1256, OECD Publishing, Paris, http://dx.doi.org/10.1787/5jrw21ntclwc-en.

Chapple, S. (2013), "Forward Liability and Welfare Reform in New Zealand", in *Policy Quarterly*, Volume 9, Issue 2.

Chenery, V. (2013), "An Evaluation of the Statement of Fitness for Work: A Survey of Employees", *DWP Research Report*, No. 840, London.

Cipollone, A., E. Pattichini and G. Vallanti (2013), "Women Labor Market Participation in Europe: Novel Evidence on Trends and Shaping Factors", *IZA Discussion Paper*, No. 7710, Bonn, http://ftp.iza.org/dp7710.pdf.

Commonwealth of Australia (2015), "2015 Intergenerational Report: Australia in 2055", The Treasury, Canberra, www.treasury.gov.au/PublicationsAndMedia/Publications/2015/2015-Intergenerational-Report.

Department of Employment (2014a), "Request for Tender – For Employment Services 2015-2020", Australian Government, https://docs.employment.gov.au/documents/request-tender-employment-services-2015-2020.

Department of Employment (2014b), "Submission to the Senate Education and Employment Legislation: Committee Inquiry into the Social Security Legislation Amendment (Strengthening the Job Seeker Compliance Framework) Bill 2014", Submission 5.

Department of Social Protection of Ireland (2016a), "One Parent Family Payment", www.welfare.ie/en/Pages/278_One-Parent-Family-Payment.aspx (accessed on 15 November 2016).

Department of Social Protection of Ireland (2016b), "After-school Child Care Scheme", www.welfare.ie/en/Pages/After-school-Child-Care-Scheme.aspx (accessed on 15 November 2016).

De Jong, P., T. Everhardt and C. Schrijvershof (2011), *Toepassing van de wet Verbetering Poortwachter* [Application of the Gatekeeper Improvement Act], APE, The Hague.

Duell, N. et al. (2010), "Activation Policies in Japan", *OECD Social, Employment and Migration Working Papers*, No. 113, OECD Publishing, Paris, http://dx.doi.org/10.1787/5km35m63qqvc-en.

Egger-Subotitsch, A. and M. Stark (2013), *Fit2work Implementierungsevaluierung* [Evaluation of the implementation of fit2work], Bundessozialamt, Vienna.

Employment and Social Development Canada (2014), "Summative Evaluation of the Targeted Initiative for Older Workers", Final Report, Partnership Evaluation, Evaluation Directorate Strategic Policy and Research Branch, 5 May.

Eurofound (2016), *The gender employment gap: Challenges and solutions*, Publications Office of the European Union, Luxembourg.

Euroguidance Denmark (2014), Guidance in Education – The Educational Guidance System in Denmark, Danish Agency for Higher Education, Copenhagen.

Federal Employment Agency of Germany [Bundesagentur für Arbeit] (2016), "Strukturen der Arbeitslosigkeit und Hilfebedürftigkeit von Alleinerziehenden [Structures of unemployment and the need for assistance of lone parents]", June, https://statistik.arbeitsagentur.de/Navigation/Statistik/Statistik-nach-Themen/Grundsicherung-fuer-Arbeitsuchende-SGBII/Personengruppen-Bedarfsgemeinschaften/Personengruppen-Bedarfsgemeinschaften-Nav.html.

Federal Ministry of Labour and Social Affairs [Bundesministerium für Arbeit und Soziales] (2013), "Alleinerziehende unterstützen – Fachkräfte gewinnen [Supporting lone parents – attracting skilled workers]", www.bmas.de/DE/Service/Medien/Publikationen/a858-alleinerziehende.html.

Federal Statistical Office of Germany [Statistisches Bundesamt] (2010), "Alleinerziehende in Deutschland: Ergebnisse des Mikrozensus 2009 [Lone parents in Germany: results of the micro census 2009]", Supplementary material for the press conference on 29 July, Wiesbaden, www.destatis.de/DE/Publikationen/Thematisch/Bevoelkerung/HaushalteMikrozensus/Alleinerziehende.html.

Federal Statistical Office of Germany [Statistisches Bundesamt] (2016), "Bevölkerung und Erwerbstätigkeit, Haushalte und Familien: Ergebnisse des Mikrozensus, 2015 [Population and employment, households and families: results of the microcensus, 2015]", Wiesbaden, www.destatis.de/GPStatistik/receive/DESerie_serie_00000209.

Fok, Y. K. and D. McVicar, Duncan (2013), "Did the 2007 welfare reforms for low income parents in Australia increase welfare exits?", in *IZA Journal of Labor Policy*, Vol. 2, http://dx.doi.org/10.1186/2193-9004-2-3.

Geyer, J., P. Haan and K. Wrohlich (2015), "The effects of family policy on maternal labor supply: Combining evidence from a structural model and a quasi-experimental approach", in *Labour Economics*, Vol. 36, http://dx.doi.org/10.1016/j.labeco.2015.07.001.

Givord, P. and C.Marbot (2015), "Does the cost of child care affect female labor market participation? An evaluation of a French reform of childcare subsidies", in *Labour Economics*, Vol. 36, October, http://dx.doi.org/10.1016/j.labeco.2015.07.003.

Goldman, L. (2015), "The Canadian targeted Initiative for Older Workers (TIOW)", OECD LEED Expert Roundtable: Local economic strategies for ageing labour markets, 31 March, http://www.oecd.org/cfe/leed/roundtable-ageing-labour-markets.htm.

Gong, X. and R. Breunig (2014), "Channels of Labour Supply Responses of Lone Parents to Changed Work Incentives", in *Oxford Economic Papers*, Vol. 66, No. 4, http://dx.doi.org/10.1093/oep/gpu022.

Greenberg, D.; J. Walter and G. Knight (2013), "A cost-benefit analysis of the random assignment UK Employment Retention and Advancement Demonstration", in *Applied Economics*, Vol. 45, No. 31, http://dx.doi.org/10.1080/00036846.2013.776664.

Hicks, P. (2015), "Local economic strategies for ageing labour markets: The Canadian Targeted Initiative for Older Workers in Fort St. James, British Columbia", *OECD Local Economic and Employment Development (LEED) Working Papers*, 2015/03, OECD Publishing, Paris, http://dx.doi.org/10.1787/5jrnwqk5d4f7-en.

Hillage, J. et al. (2012), "Evaluation of the Fit for Work Service Pilots: First Year Report", *DWP Research Report*, No. 792, London.

HMT – Her Majesty's Treasury (2011), "The Green Book: Appraisal and Evaluation in Central Government", www.gov.uk/government/publications/the-green-book-appraisal-and-evaluation-in-central-governent.

Hullegie, P. and J.C. van Ours (2013), "Seek and ye shall find: How search requirements affect job finding rates of older workers", *IZA Discussion Paper*, No. 7400, IZA, Bonn.

Kalíšková, K. (2015), "Tax and Transfer Policies and the Female Labor Supply in the EU", *IZA Discussion Paper*, No. 8949, IZA, Bonn, http://ftp.iza.org/dp8949.pdf.

Knoef, M. and J. van Ours (2016), "How to stimulate single mothers on welfare to find a job: Evidence from a policy experiment", in *Journal of Population Economics*, Vol. 29, Issue 4, http://dx.doi.org/10.1007/s00148-016-0593-0.

Koning, P. and M. Raterink (2013), "Re-employment rates of older unemployed workers: Decomposing the effect of birth cohorts and policy changes", in *De Economist*, Vol. 161, http://dx.doi.org/10.1007/s10645-013-9208-2.

Koopmans, P., C. Roelen, and J. Groothoff (2008), "Frequent and Long-term Absence as a Risk Factor for Work Disability and Job Termination Among Employees in the Private Sector", *Occupational and Environmental Medicine*, Vol. 65, pp. 494-499.

Lammers, M., H. Bloemen and S. Hochguertel (2013), "Job search requirements for older unemployed: Transitions to employment, early retirement and disability benefits", *European Economic Review*, Vol. 58.

Langenbucher, K. (2015), "How demanding are eligibility criteria for unemployment benefits, quantitative indicators for OECD and EU countries", *OECD Social, Employment and Migration Working Papers*, No. 166, OECD Publishing, Paris, http://dx.doi.org/10.1787/5jrxtk1zw8f2-en.

Meager, N. et al. (2014), "Work Programme evaluation: The participant experience report", *Department for Work and Pensions Research Report*, No. 892, London.

Müller, K.-U. and K. Wrohlich (2016), "Two Steps Forward—One Step Back? Evaluating Contradicting Child Care Policies in Germany", in *CESifo Economic Studies*, Vol. 62, No. 4, http://dx.doi.org/10.1093/cesifo/ifv020.

New Zealand Ministry of Social Development (2016), "Effectiveness of MSD employment assistance. Summary report for 2014/2015 financial year", Wellington.

New Zealand Ministry of Social Development (2013), "The impact of the Future Focus work obligations for sole parents: Technical report", Knowledge and Insights, Ministry of Social Development, Wellington.

New Zealand Productivity Commission (2016), *More Effective Social Services*, Wellington, www.productivity.govt.nz/inquiry-content/2032?stage=4.

New Zealand Treasury (2015), "Guide to social cost benefit analysis", www.treasury.govt.nz/publications/guidance/planning/costbenefitanalysis/guide/.

OECD (*forthcoming*), "Key policies to promote longer working lives in Australia", Ageing and Employment Policies, Country Policy Monitoring.

OECD (2017), *Back to Work: New Zealand: Improving the Re-employment Prospects of Displaced Workers*, Back to Work, OECD Publishing, Paris, http://dx.doi.org/10.1787/23063831.

OECD (2016a), *Investing in Youth: Australia*, Investing in Youth, OECD Publishing, Paris, http://dx.doi.org/10.1787/9789264257498-en.

OECD (2016b), *Back to Work: Australia: Improving the Re-employment Prospects of Displaced Workers*, Back to Work, OECD Publishing, Paris, http://dx.doi.org/10.1787/9789264253476-en.

OECD (2016c), *Back to Work: Denmark: Improving the Re-employment Prospects of Displaced Workers*, Back to Work, OECD Publishing, Paris, http://dx.doi.org/10.1787/23063831.

OECD (2016d), "Recommendation of the Council on aging and employment policies", Paris, www.oecd.org/employment/ministerial/labour-ministerial-statement-2016.pdf.

OECD (2016e), *Society at a Glance 2016: OECD Social Indicators*, OECD Publishing, Paris, http://dx.doi.org/10.1787/9789264261488-en.

OECD (2016f), *Investing in Youth: Sweden*, Investing in Youth, OECD Publishing, Paris, http://dx.doi.org/10.1787/9789264267701-en.

OECD (2016g), *Recommendation of the Council on Integrated Mental Health, Skills and Work Policy*, Paris, www.oecd.org/employment/ministerial/labour-ministerial-statement-2016.pdf.

OECD (2016h), *Dare to Share: Germany's Experience Promoting Equal Partnership in Families*, OECD Publishing, Paris, http://dx.doi.org/10.1787/9789264259157-en.

OECD (2015a), "Activation policies for more inclusive labour markets", in *OECD Employment Outlook 2015*, OECD Publishing, Paris, http://dx.doi.org/10.1787/empl_outlook-2015-7-en.

OECD (2015b), *Back to Work: Canada: Improving the Re-employment Prospects of Displaced Workers*, Back to Work, OECD Publishing, Paris, http://dx.doi.org/10.1787/9789264233454-en.

OECD (2015c), *Back to Work: Sweden: Improving the Re-employment Prospects of Displaced Workers*, Back to Work, OECD Publishing, Paris, http://dx.doi.org/10.1787/23063831.

OECD (2015d), *Mental Health and Work: Austria*, OECD Publishing, Paris, http://dx.doi.org/10.1787/9789264228047-en.

OECD (2015e), *Fit Mind, Fit Job: From Evidence to Practice in Mental Health and Work*, OECD Publishing, Paris, http://dx.doi.org/10.1787/9789264228283-en.

OECD (2015f), *Mental Health and Work: Australia*, Mental Health and Work, OECD Publishing, Paris, http://dx.doi.org/10.1787/9789264246591-en.

OECD (2015g), *Starting Strong IV: Monitoring Quality in Early Childhood Education and Care*, OECD Publishing, Paris, http://dx.doi.org/10.1787/9789264233515-en.

OECD (2014a), *Connecting People with Jobs: Activation Policies in the United Kingdom*, OECD Publishing, Paris, http://dx.doi.org/10.1787/9789264217188-en.

OECD (2014b), *Ageing and Employment Policies: Netherlands 2014: Working Better with Age*, OECD Publishing, Paris, http://dx.doi.org/10.1787/9789264208155-en.

OECD (2014c), *Mental Health and Work: Switzerland*, OECD Publishing, Paris, http://dx.doi.org/10.1787/9789264204973-en;

OECD (2014d), "New Zealand 2014", Country specific information for the OECD series *Benefits and Wages* www.oecd.org/els/social/workincentives.

OECD (2014e), "Denmark 2014", Country specific information for the OECD series *Benefits and Wages* www.oecd.org/els/social/workincentives.

OECD (2014f), *Mental Health and Work: Netherlands*, OECD Publishing, Paris, http://dx.doi.org/10.1787/9789264223301-en.

OECD (2013a), *Mental Health and Work: United Kingdom*, OECD Publishing, Paris, http://dx.doi.org/10.1787/9789264204997-en.

OECD (2013b), *Mental Health and Work: Denmark*, OECD Publishing, Paris, http://dx.doi.org/10.1787/9789264188631-en;

OECD (2013c), *Mental Health and Work: Sweden*, OECD Publishing, Paris, http://dx.doi.org/10.1787/9789264188730-en .

OECD (2013d), *Mental Health and Work: Belgium*, OECD Publishing, Paris, http://dx.doi.org/10.1787/9789264187566-en.

OECD (2012a), *Activating Jobseekers: How Australia Does It*, OECD Publishing, Paris, http://dx.doi.org/10.1787/9789264185920-en.

OECD (2012b), *Sick on the Job? Myths and Realities about Mental Health and Work*, OECD Publishing, Paris, http://dx.doi.org/10.1787/9789264124523-en.

OECD (2011), *Doing Better for Families*, OECD Publishing, Paris, http://dx.doi.org/10.1787/9789264098732-en.

OECD (2010), *Sickness, Disability and Work: Breaking the Barriers – A Synthesis of Findings across OECD Countries*, OECD Publishing, Paris, http://dx.doi.org/10.1787/9789264088856-en.

OECD (2003), *Transforming Disability into Ability: Policies to Promote Work and Income Security for Disabled People*, OECD Publishing, Paris, http://dx.doi.org/10.1787/9789264158245-en.

Pareliussen, J.K. (2013), "Work Incentives and Universal Credit: Reform of the benefit system in the United Kingdom", *OECD Economics Department Working Papers*, No. 1033, OECD Publishing, Paris, http://dx.doi.org/10.1787/5k49lcn89rkf-en.

PricewaterhouseCoopers (2016), Valuation Report 30 June 2015, Baseline Valuation, Report prepared for the Department of Social Services, Canberra, https://www.dss.gov.au/sites/default/files/documents/09_2016/baseline_valuation_results_report_accessible_version_12_july_2016_2pwc._2.pdf.

Productivity Commission (2014), "Childcare and Early Childhood Learning: Overview", *Inquiry Report*, No. 73, Canberra.

Senior Labour Inspectors Committee (2008), "Report on the Evaluation of the Danish Working Environment Authority in 2008", Copenhagen;

Service public fédéral Emploi, Travail et Concertation sociale (2011), Évaluation de la législation relative à la prévention de la charge psychosociale occasionnée par le travail, dont la violence et le harcèlement moral ou sexuel au travail, Brussels.

Shiels, C. et al. (2013), "An Evaluation of the Statement of Fitness for Work: Quantitative Survey of Fit Notes", *DWP Research Report*, No. 841, London.

Skaner, Y. et al. (2011), "Use and Usefulness of Guidelines for Sickness Certification: Results from a National Survey of All General Practitioners in Sweden", *BMJ Open*, Vol. 1, No. 1.

The Danish Government (2013), The National Reform Programme Denmark 2013, Copenhagen.

The Danish Government (2012), The National Reform Programme Denmark 2012, Copenhagen.

Thévenon, O. (2015), "Do 'Institutional Complementarities' Foster Female Labour Force Participation?", in *Journal of Institutional Economics*, Vol. 12, No. 2, pp. 471-497, June, http://dx.doi.org/10.1017/S1744137415000399.

Thévenon, O. (2013), "Drivers of Female Labour Force Participation in the OECD", *OECD Social, Employment and Migration Working Papers*, No. 145, OECD Publishing. Paris, http://dx.doi.org/10.1787/5k46cvrgnms6-en.

The Treasury (2016), "Budget 2016-17: Budget Measures", Budget Paper No. 2, Canberra, www.budget.gov.au/2016-17/content/.

The Treasury (2015a), "Budget 2015-16: Budget Measures", Budget Paper No. 2, Canberra, www.budget.gov.au/2015-16/.

The Treasury (2015b), "Budget 2015-16: Families Package", Canberra, www.budget.gov.au/2015-16/.

Database references

OECD Database on Labour Market Programmes, Public expenditure of LMP by main categories (% of GDP), http://dx.doi.org/10.1787/data-00312-en.

OECD Family Database, The labour market position of families, LMF1.3 Maternal employment by partnership status, http://www.oecd.org/social/family/database.htm.

ORGANISATION FOR ECONOMIC CO-OPERATION AND DEVELOPMENT

The OECD is a unique forum where governments work together to address the economic, social and environmental challenges of globalisation. The OECD is also at the forefront of efforts to understand and to help governments respond to new developments and concerns, such as corporate governance, the information economy and the challenges of an ageing population. The Organisation provides a setting where governments can compare policy experiences, seek answers to common problems, identify good practice and work to co-ordinate domestic and international policies.

The OECD member countries are: Australia, Austria, Belgium, Canada, Chile, the Czech Republic, Denmark, Estonia, Finland, France, Germany, Greece, Hungary, Iceland, Ireland, Israel, Italy, Japan, Korea, Latvia, Luxembourg, Mexico, the Netherlands, New Zealand, Norway, Poland, Portugal, the Slovak Republic, Slovenia, Spain, Sweden, Switzerland, Turkey, the United Kingdom and the United States. The European Union takes part in the work of the OECD.

OECD Publishing disseminates widely the results of the Organisation's statistics gathering and research on economic, social and environmental issues, as well as the conventions, guidelines and standards agreed by its members.

OECD PUBLISHING, 2, rue André-Pascal, 75775 PARIS CEDEX 16
(81 2017 04 1 P) ISBN 978-92-64-26962-0 – 2017

www.ingramcontent.com/pod-product-compliance
Lightning Source LLC
LaVergne TN
LVHW081410110826
845149LV00010B/1692

* 9 7 8 9 2 6 4 2 6 9 6 2 0 *